Plant-Based Cookbook for Be

Mouth-Watering, Affordable, Vegan, Healthy, Delicious Recipes for Your Conscious Diet.

Introduction 6

Breakfast 7

1. Almond Plum Oats Overnight 7
2. High Protein Toast 7
3. Hummus Carrot Sandwich 8
4. Avocado Miso Chickpeas Toast 8
5. Banana Malt Bread 8
6. Banana Vegan Bread 9
7. Berry Compote Pancakes 9
8. Southwest Breakfast Bowl 10
9. Buckwheat Crepes 10
10. Chickpeas Spread Sourdough Toast ... 10
11. Chickpeas with Harissa 11
12. Quinoa Quiche Cups 11
13. French toast 11
14. Blueberry-Banana Muffins 11
15. Apple Pie Oat Bowls 12
16. Hash Browns 12
17. Apple-Cinnamon Breakfast Cookies .. 12
18. Cinnamon Rolls 13
19. Tofu Scramble Brunch Bowls 13
20. PB and J Power Tarts 13
21. Avocado Bagels 14
22. Samosa Rolls 14
23. Tofu-Spinach Scramble 15
24. Savory Pancakes 15
25. English Muffins with Tofu 16
26. Multigrain Hot Cereal with Apricots .. 16
27. Cinnamon Pear Oatmeal 16
28. Hearty Pineapple Oatmeal 17
29. Cool Mushroom Munchies 17
30. Delightful Berry Quinoa Bowl 17
31. Cinnamon-Banana French Toast 18
32. Frosty Hemp and Blackberry Smoothie Bowl 18
33. Chocolate and Walnut Steel-Cut Oats 18
34. Traditional Indian Roti 19
35. Chocolate Chia Pudding 19
36. Easy Morning Polenta 19
37. Mixed Berry and Almond Butter Swirl Bowl 19
38. Everyday Oats with Coconut and Strawberries 20
39. The Best Chocolate Granola Ever 20
40. Autumn Pumpkin Griddle Cakes 21
41. Cinnamon Semolina Porridge 21
42. Decadent Applesauce French Toast ... 21
43. Nutty Morning Bread Pudding 22
44. Moroccan Lentil and Raisin Salad 22
45. Pumpkin Oatmeal 22
46. Cauliflower Oatmeal 23
47. Hemp Breakfast Cookies 23
48. Zucchini Oatmeal 23
49. Peanut Butter Muffins 24
50. Chocolate Zucchini Bread 24

Lunch 25

51. French Onion Soup 25
52. Lasagna Soup 25
53. Black Bean and Mushroom Stew 26
54. Spicy Peanut Ramen 26
55. Creamy Mushroom Soup 26
56. Potato Harvest Stew 27
57. Quick Black Bean Chili 27
58. Sweet Potato and Peanut Stew 27
59. Split Pea Soup 28
60. Sour Soup 28
61. Roasted Tomato Soup 29
62. Butternut Squash 29
63. Wonton Soup 30
64. Potato and Kale Soup 30
65. Ramen Soup 30
66. Vegetable and Barley Stew 31
67. Vegan Pho 31
68. Garden Vegetable Stew 32
69. Moroccan Vegetable Stew 32

70.	Matzo Ball Soup	33
71.	White Bean and Broccoli Salad	33
72.	Chinese Black Bean Chili	34
73.	Coconut Rice	34
74.	Baked Beans	34
75.	Lemony Quinoa	35
76.	Vegan Curried Rice	35
77.	Spicy Cabbage Salad	35
78.	Wholesome Farm Salad	36
79.	Spicy Chickpea Crunch	36
80.	Easy Italian Bowl	37
81.	Light Lemon Salad	37
82.	Cooked Cauliflower Bowl	37
83.	Seasoned Tofu Potato Salad	38
84.	Classic Potato Comfort	38
85.	Fried Zucchini	39
86.	Thick Sweet Potato Fries	39
87.	Hot Wings with Ranch	40
88.	Breaded Tempeh Bites	40
89.	Cumin Chili Chickpeas	41
90.	Summer Sushi	41
91.	Special Cheese Board	41
92.	Three-Ingredient Flatbread	42
93.	Spicy Homemade Tortilla Chips	42
94.	Healthy Cereal Bars	42
95.	Black Bean Taquitos	43
96.	Vegetable Tacos	43
97.	Tomato Basil Soup	44
98.	Pearl Couscous Salad	44
99.	Vegan Tomato Soup	44
100.	Butternut Squash Chickpea Stew	45
Dinner		46
101.	Sweet and Sour Tempeh	46
102.	Fried Seitan Fingers	46
103.	Crusty Grilled Corn	47
104.	Grilled Carrots with Chickpea Salad	47
105.	Grilled Avocado Guacamole	47
106.	Spinach and Dill Pasta Salad	48
107.	Italian Veggie Salad	48
108.	Spinach and Mashed Tofu Salad	49
109.	Super Summer Salad	49
110.	Roasted Almond Protein Salad	49
111.	Lentil, Lemon and Mushroom Salad	50
112.	Sweet Potato and Black Bean Protein Salad	50
113.	Lentil Radish Salad	51
114.	Jicama and Spinach Salad Recipe	51
115.	High-Protein Salad	52
116.	Mussels in Red Wine Sauce	52
117.	Roast Balsamic Vegetables	52
118.	Vegan Caesar Salad	53
119.	Steak and Mushroom Noodles	54
120.	Masala Scallops	54
121.	Lemongrass and Ginger Mackerel	54
122.	Mashed Potatoes	54
123.	Quinoa with Vegetables	55
124.	Cold Cauliflower-Coconut Soup	55
125.	Lettuce Bean Burritos	55
126.	Mango Chutney Wraps	56
127.	Chickpea Fajitas	56
128.	Garlic and White Bean Soup	57
129.	Quinoa and Chickpeas Salad	57
130.	Pecan Rice	57
131.	Barley Bake	58
132.	Black Beans, Corn, and Yellow Rice	58
133.	Black Beans and Rice	58
134.	Vegetable and Chickpea Loaf	59
135.	Thyme and Lemon Couscous	59
136.	Pesto and White Bean Pasta	59
137.	Baked Okra and Tomato	60
138.	Bean and Carrot Spirals	60
139.	Tofu Nuggets with Barbecue Glaze	60
140.	Peppered Pinto Beans	60
141.	Chili Fennel	61

#	Recipe	Page
142.	Cajun and Balsamic Okra	61
143.	Cashew Zucchinis	61
144.	Cauliflower Gnocchi	62
145.	Curry Chickpea	62
146.	Grilled Margherita	63
147.	Vegan Moroccan Stew	63
148.	Lime Bean Artichoke Wraps	64
149.	Butternut Squash Lasagna	64
150.	Broccoli Dip	65

Snack 66

#	Recipe	Page
151.	Smoky Red Pepper Hummus	66
152.	Roasted Tamari Almonds	66
153.	Tomatillo Salsa	67
154.	Arugula Pesto Couscous	67
155.	Oatmeal and Raisin Balls	67
156.	Oat Crunch Apple Crisp	68
157.	Pico de Gallo	68
158.	Beet Balls	68
159.	Cheesy Crackers	69
160.	Chocolate Protein Bites	69
161.	Crunchy Granola	69
162.	Chocolate Almond Bars	70
163.	Spicy Nut and Seed Snack Mix	70
164.	Flax Crackers	70
165.	Chocolate and Nuts Goji Bars	71
166.	Cranberry Protein Bars	71
167.	Onion Rings	71
168.	French Fries	72
169.	Roasted Asparagus	72
170.	Twice-Baked Potatoes	72
171.	Baba Ghanoush	73
172.	Citrus-Roasted Brussels sprouts	73
173.	Berry and Yogurt Smoothie	73
174.	Basil Lime Green Tea	73
175.	Pineapple and Spinach Juice	74
176.	Strawberry and Chocolate Milkshake	74
177.	Fruit Infused Water	74
178.	Lebanese Potato Salad	74
179.	Kale and Cauliflower Salad	75
180.	Creamy Lentil Dip	75
181.	Easy Cucumber Dip	75
182.	Ranch Cauliflower Dip	76
183.	Sweet and Tangy Ketchup	76
184.	Cilantro Coconut Pesto	76
185.	Raw Cashew Pesto	76
186.	Plantain Chips	77
187.	Stuffed Portobello	77
188.	Easy Collard Greens	77
189.	Sesame Fries	78
190.	French Potato Salad	78
191.	Vanilla Milk Steamer	78
192.	Cannellini Pesto Spaghetti	79
193.	Cold Orange Soba Noodles	79
194.	Indonesia Green Noodle Salad	79
195.	Fruity Rice Pudding	79
196.	Oat Cookies	80
197.	Sweet Potato Tater Tots	80
198.	Roasted Pepper and Tomato Dip	80
199.	Seeds Crackers	81
200.	Spicy Almonds	81

Dessert 82

#	Recipe	Page
201.	Berries Pie	82
202.	Vanilla and Apple Brownies	82
203.	Banana Cake	83
204.	Coconut Mousse	83
205.	Mango Coconut Pudding	83
206.	Rhubarb and Berries Pie	83
207.	Banana Salad	84
208.	Lemon Berries	84
209.	Peach Stew	84
210.	Apple Stew	84
211.	Minty Apricots	85
212.	Mango Mix	85
213.	Blueberry Stew	85

214.	Lime Cream 85	235.	Vanilla Flavored Whole Grain Muffins 92
215.	Vanilla Peach Mix 86	236.	Coconut Banana Sandwich with Raspberry Spread 92
216.	Pear Stew 86	237.	Apple Toasted Sweet Sandwich 93
217.	Mango Shake 86	238.	Dried Cranberry Almond Bowl 93
218.	Lime Bars 86	239.	Chocolate Banana Breakfast Bowl 94
219.	Blackberry Cobbler 87	240.	Fresh mint and coconut Fruit Salad ... 94
220.	Black Tea Cake 87	241.	Nutty Fruity Breakfast Bowl 94
221.	Green Tea Avocado Pudding ... 87	242.	Peppery Mushroom Tomato Bowl 95
222.	Pineapple and Mango Oatmeal 87	243.	Roasted Beets and Carrot with Avocado Dip 95
223.	Breakfast Quinoa 88	244.	Raisin Oat Cookies 96
224.	Strawberry Chia Jam 88	245.	Oat Scones 96
225.	Sticky Rice Congee with Dates 88	246.	Golden Milk 97
226.	Easy Apple and Cinnamon Muesli 89	247.	Mango Agua Fresca 97
227.	Salted Caramel Oatmeal 89	248.	Classic Switchel 97
228.	Creamy Brown Rice Cereal with Raisins 89	249.	Easy and Fresh Mango Madness 97
229.	Cashew-Date Waffles 89	250.	Blueberry Coconut Milkshake 98
230.	Maple Sunflower Seed Granola 90	Index 99	
231.	Vegan Dairy Free Breakfast Bowl 90	Conclusion 102	
232. Nuts	Hot and Healthy Breakfast Bowl with 91		
233.	Healthy Chocolate Oats Bites 91		
234.	Homemade Nutty Fruity Muffins 91		

Introduction

A plant-based diet consists primarily of plant-based foods such as fruits and vegetables, as well as nuts, whole grains, legumes and seeds.

It is not a vegetarian or vegan diet because it is possible to eat poultry, beef, eggs, fish, and dairy products, but plant-based foods provide the majority of your nutrient intake. On a plant-based diet, there is no set ratio of plant to animal foods, but eating at least 70% of vegetables is a good place to start. The focus should be on plants.

Is it healthy to eat a plant-based diet?
Yes. A plant-based diet is nutrient-dense and high in protein, vitamins, fiber, minerals, and healthy fats. It is considered a very healthy way of eating and can meet all of your nutritional requirements.

Who should follow a plant-based diet?
A plant-based diet can benefit the majority of adults. According to research, plant-based diets can help prevent and treat chronic diseases, as well as reduce reliance on medications. If you have a medical condition, talk to your doctor before changing your diet.

How does a plant-based diet provide enough protein?
Avoid associating protein with meat. Tofu, lentils, beans, nuts and nut butters, seeds, and quinoa are all excellent plant-based protein sources. Remember that dairy, eggs, beef, poultry, and fish are all acceptable on a plant-based diet; they just shouldn't be the main course.

How does one begin a plant-based diet?
Starting a plant-based diet may seem overwhelming at first, but take it one day at a time.
You can do like this:
1. Consume a lot of vegetables. At lunch and dinner, make half of your plate vegetables. When selecting vegetables, make sure to include a variety of colors. Snack on vegetables with hummus, salsa, or guacamole.
2. Modify your attitude toward meat. Have smaller portions and do not consider it the main course anymore.
3. Choose healthy fats. Healthy fats can be found in olive oil, olives, nuts and nut butters, seeds, and avocados.
4. At least once a week, cook a vegetarian meal. Prepare these meals with beans, whole grains, and vegetables.
5. Eat whole grains for breakfast. Begin with a grain such as oatmeal, quinoa, buckwheat, or barley. Then top with nuts or seeds and fresh fruit.
6. Opt for greens. Every day, eat a variety of green leafy vegetables like kale, collards, Swiss chard, spinach, and other greens. To retain flavor and nutrients, steam, grill, braise, or stir-fry them.
7. Create a meal around a salad. In a bowl, combine salad greens such as romaine, spinach, Bibb, or red leafy greens. Mix in a variety of other vegetables, fresh herbs, beans, peas, or tofu.
8. For dessert, eat fruit. After a meal, a ripe, juicy peach, a refreshing slice of watermelon, or a crisp apple will satisfy your sweet tooth.

Should there be any plants avoided on a plant-based diet?
A plant-based diet can include any plant.

Breakfast

1. Almond Plum Oats Overnight

Preparation time: 15-30 Minutes
Cooking time: 0 Minutes
Servings: 1

Ingredients:
- Rolled oats: 60g
- Plums: 3 ripe and chopped
- Almond milk: 300ml
- Chia seeds: 1 tbsp.
- Nutmeg: a pinch
- Vanilla extract: a few drops
- Whole almonds: 1 tbsp. roughly chopped

Directions:
1. Add oats, nutmeg, vanilla extract, almond milk, and chia seeds to a bowl and mix well
2. Add in cubed plums and cover and place in the fridge for a night
3. Mix the oats well next morning and add into the serving bowl
4. Serve with your favorite toppings

Nutrition:
Calories: 248 Carbohydrates: 24.7g Proteins: 9.5g Fat: 10.8g

2. High Protein Toast

Preparation time: 30 Minutes
Cooking time: 0 Minutes
Servings: 1

Ingredients:
- White bean: 1 drained and rinsed
- Cashew cream: ½ cup
- Miso paste: 1 ½ tbsp.
- Toasted sesame oil: 1 tsp.
- Sesame seeds: 1 tbsp.
- Spring onion: 1 finely sliced
- Lemon: 1 half for the juice and half wedged to serve
- Rye bread: 4 slices toasted

Directions:
1. In a bowl add sesame oil, white beans, miso, cashew cream, and lemon juice and mash using a potato masher
2. Make a spread
3. Spread it on a toast and top with spring onions and sesame seeds
4. Serve with lemon wedges

Nutrition:
Calories: 332 Carbohydrates: 44.5g Proteins: 14.5g Fat: 9.25g

3. Hummus Carrot Sandwich

Preparation time: 30 Minutes   Cooking time: 15 Minutes   Servings: 1

Ingredients:
- Chickpeas: 1 cup can drain and rinsed
- Tomato: 1 small sliced
- Cucumber: 1 sliced
- Avocado: 1 sliced
- Cumin: 1 tsp.
- Carrot: 1 cup diced
- Maple syrup: 1 tsp.
- Tahini: 3 tbsp.
- Garlic: 1 clove
- Lemon: 2 tbsp.
- Extra-virgin olive oil: 2 tbsp.
- Salt: as per your need
- Bread slices: 4

Directions:
1. Add carrot to the boiling hot water and boil for 15 minutes
2. Blend boiled carrots, maple syrup, cumin, chickpeas, tahini, olive oil, salt, and garlic together in a blender
3. Add in lemon juice and mix
4. Add to the serving bowl and you can refrigerate for up to 5 days
5. In between two bread slices, spread hummus and place 2-3 slices of cucumber, avocado, and tomato and serve

Nutrition:
Calories: 490 Carbohydrates: 53.15g Proteins: 14.1g Fat: 27g

4. Avocado Miso Chickpeas Toast

Preparation time: 30 Minutes   Cooking time: 15 Minutes   Servings: 1

Ingredients:
- Chickpeas: 400g drained and rinsed
- Avocado: 1 medium
- Toasted sesame oil: 1 tsp.
- White miso paste: 1 ½ tbsp.
- Sesame seeds: 1 tbsp.
- Spring onion: 1 finely sliced
- Lemon: 1 half for the juice and half wedged to serve
- Rye bread: 4 slices toasted

Directions:
1. In a bowl add sesame oil, chickpeas, miso, and lemon juice and mash using a potato masher
2. Roughly crushed avocado in another bowl using a fork
3. Add the avocado to the chickpeas and make a spread
4. Spread it on a toast and top with spring onion and sesame seeds
5. Serve with lemon wedges

Nutrition:
Calories: 456 Carbohydrates: 13.3g Proteins: 14.6g Fat: 26.6g

5. Banana Malt Bread

Preparation time: 30 Minutes   **Cooking time:** 1 Hour and 20 Minutes   Servings: 1

Ingredients:
- Hot strong black tea: 120ml
- Malt extract: 150g plus extra for brushing
- Bananas: 2 ripe mashed
- Sultanas: 100g

- Pitted dates: 120g chopped
- Plain flour: 250g
- Soft dark brown sugar: 50g
- Baking powder: 2 tsp.

Directions:
1. Preheat the oven to 140C
2. Line the loaf tin with the baking paper
3. Brew tea and include sultanas and dates to it
4. Take a small pan and heat the malt extract and gradually add sugar to it
5. Stir continuously and let it cook
6. In a bowl, attach flour, salt, and baking powder and now top with sugar extract, fruits, bananas, and tea
7. Mix the batter well and add to the loaf tin
8. Bake the mixture for an hour
9. Brush the bread with extra malt extract and let it cool down before removing from the tin
10. When done, wrap in a foil; it can be consumed for a week

Nutrition:
Calories: 194 Carbohydrates: 43.3g Proteins: 3.4g Fat: 0.3g

6. Banana Vegan Bread

Preparation time: 30 Minutes   **Cooking time:** 1 Hour and 15 Minutes   Servings: 1

Ingredients:
- Overripe banana:
- 3 largest mashed
- All-purpose flour: 200 g
- Unsweetened non-dairy milk: 50 ml
- White vinegar: ½ tsp.
- Ground flaxseed: 10 g
- Ground cinnamon: ¼ tsp.
- Granulated sugar: 140 g
- Vanilla: ¼ tsp.
- Baking powder: ¼ tsp.
- Baking soda: ¼ tsp.
- Salt: ¼ tsp.
- Canola oil: 3 tbsp.
- Chopped walnuts: ½ cup

Directions:
1. Warmth the oven to 350F and line the loaf pan with parchment paper
2. Mash bananas using a fork
3. Take a large bowl, and add in mash bananas, canola oil, oat milk, sugar, vinegar, vanilla, and ground flax seed
4. Also whisk in baking powder, cinnamon, flour, and salt
5. Attach battery to the loaf pan and bake for 50 minutes
6. Remove from pan and let it sit for 10 minutes
7. Slice when completely cooled down

Nutrition:
Calories: 240 Carbohydrates: 40.3g Proteins: 2.8g Fat: 8.2g

7. Berry Compote Pancakes

Preparation time: 30 Minutes   **Cooking time:** 13-14 Minutes   Servings: 1

Ingredients:
- Mixed frozen berries: 200g
- Plain flour: 140 g
- Unsweetened almond milk: 140ml
- Icing sugar: 1 tbsp.
- Lemon juice: 1 tbsp.
- Baking powder: 2 tsp.
- Vanilla extract: a dash
- Salt: a pinch
- Caster sugar: 2 tbsp.
- Vegetable oil: ½ tbsp.

Directions:
1. Take a small pan and add berries, lemon juice, and icing sugar
2. Cook the mixture for 10 minutes to give it a saucy texture and set aside
3. Take a bowl and add caster sugar, flour, baking powder, and salt and mix well

4. Add in almond milk and vanilla and combine well to make a batter
5. Take a non-stick pan, and heat 2 teaspoons oil in it and spread it over the whole surface
6. Attach ¼ cup of the batter to the pan and cook each side for 3-4 minutes
7. Serve with compote

Nutrition:
Calories: 463 Carbohydrates: 92g Proteins: 9.4g Fat: 5.2g

8. Southwest Breakfast Bowl

Preparation time: 30 Minutes   Cooking time: 0 minutes   Servings: 1

Ingredients:
- Mushrooms: 1 cup sliced
- Chopped cilantro: ½ cup
- Chili powder: 1 tsp.
- Red pepper: ½ diced
- Zucchini: 1 cup diced
- Green onion: ½ cup chopped
- Onion: ½ cup
- Vegan sausage: 1 sliced
- Garlic powder: 1 tsp.
- Paprika: 1 tsp.
- Cumin: ½ tsp.
- Salt and pepper: as per your taste
- Avocado: for topping

Directions:
1. Put everything in a bowl and apply gentle heat until vegetables turn brown
2. Pour some pepper and salt as you like and serve with your favorite toppings

Nutrition:
Calories: 361 Carbohydrates: 31.6g Proteins: 33.8g Fat: 12.2g

9. Buckwheat Crepes

Preparation time: 30 Minutes   Cooking time: 25 Minutes   Servings: 1

Ingredients:
- Raw buckwheat flour: 1 cup
- Light coconut milk: 1 and ¾ cups
- Ground cinnamon: ⅛ tsp.
- Flaxseeds: ¾ tbsp.
- Melted coconut oil: 1 tbsp.
- Sea salt: a pinch
- Any sweetener: as per your taste

Directions:
1. Take a bowl and add flaxseed, coconut milk, salt, avocado, and cinnamon
2. Mix them all well and fold in the flour
3. Now take a nonstick pan and pour oil and provide gentle heat
4. Add a big spoon of a mixture
5. Cook till it appears bubbly, and then change side
6. Perform the task until all crepes are prepared
7. For enhancing the taste, add the sweetener of your liking

Nutrition:
Calories: 71 Carbohydrates: 8g Proteins: 1g Fat: 3g

10. Chickpeas Spread Sourdough Toast

Preparation time: 30 Minutes   Cooking time: 0 Minutes   Servings: 1

Ingredients:
- Chickpeas: 1 cup rinsed and drained
- Pumpkin puree: 1 cup
- Vegan yogurt: ½ cup
- Salt: as per your need
- Sourdough: 2 slices toasted

Directions:
1. In a bowl add chickpeas and pumpkin puree and mash using a potato masher
2. Add in salt and yogurt and mix
3. Spread it on a toast and serve

Nutrition:
Calories: 187 Carbohydrates: 33.7g Proteins: 8.45g Fat: 2.5g

11. Chickpeas with Harissa

Preparation time: 30 Minutes   Cooking time: 0 Minutes   Servings: 1

Ingredients:
- Chickpeas: 1 cup can rinse and drained well
- Onion: 1 small diced
- Cucumber: 1 cup diced
- Tomato: 1 cup diced
- Salt: as per your taste
- Lemon juice: 2 tbsp.
- Harissa: 2 tsp.
- Olive oil: 1 tbsp.
- Flat-leaf parsley
- 2 tbsp. chopped

Directions:
1. Add lemon juice, harissa, and olive oil in a bowl and whisk
2. Take a serving bowl and add onion, cucumber, chickpeas, salt and the sauce you made
3. Add parsley from the top and serve

Nutrition:
Calories: 398 Carbohydrates: 55.6g Proteins: 17.8g Fat: 11.8g

12. Quinoa Quiche Cups

Preparation time: 5 minutes   **Cooking time:** 20 minutes   Servings: 6

Ingredients:
- 1 (10-ounce) bag frozen mixed vegetables, thawed
- ¾ cup quinoa flour
- ¾ cup water
- 2 tablespoons freshly squeezed lemon juice
- ¼ cup nutritional yeast
- ¼ teaspoon granulated garlic
- ¼ teaspoon sea salt
- Freshly ground black pepper

Directions:
1. In a medium bowl, mix the vegetables, quinoa flour, water, lemon juice, nutritional yeast, granulated garlic, salt, and pepper to taste until well combined.
2. Spoon the mixture into 6 cupcake molds, dividing it evenly.
3. Place the filled molds into the air fryer and bake at 340F for 20 minutes. Let cool slightly before enjoying.

Nutrition:
Calories: 239 Fat: 2g Carbohydrates: 39g Fiber: 8g Proteins: 16g

13. French toast

Preparation time: 5 minutes   **Cooking time:** 10 minutes   Servings: 4

Ingredients:
- 1 ripe banana, mashed
- ¼ cup protein powder
- ½ cup plant-based milk
- 2 tablespoons ground flaxseed
- 4 slices whole-grain bread
- Nonstick cooking spray

Directions:
1. In a shallow bowl, mix the banana, protein powder, plant-based milk, and flaxseed until well combined.
2. Set both sides of each slice of bread into the mixture. Lightly spray your pan or air fryer basket with oil and place the slices on it in a single layer. Pour any remaining mixture evenly over the bread.
3. Bring the pan in the air fryer and fry at 370F for 10 minutes, or until golden brown and crispy. Be sure to flip the toast over halfway through. Enjoy the warmth.

Nutrition:
Calories: 365 Fat: 11g Carbohydrates: 48g Fiber: 9g Proteins: 22g

14. Blueberry-Banana Muffins

Preparation time: 16 minutes   **Cooking time:** 16 minutes   Servings: 6

Ingredients:

- 1 ripe banana
- ½ cup unsweetened plant-based milk
- 1 teaspoon apple cider vinegar
- 1 teaspoon vanilla extract
- 2 tablespoons ground flaxseed
- 2 tablespoons coconut sugar
- ¾ cup all-purpose flour
- 1 teaspoon baking powder
- ½ teaspoon baking soda
- ¾ cup blueberries

Directions:
1. In a medium bowl, press the banana with a fork. Add the plant-based milk, apple cider vinegar, vanilla, flaxseed, and coconut sugar and mix until well combined. Set aside.
2. In a small bowl set together the flour, baking powder, and baking soda. Add this mixture to the medium bowl and mix until just combined. (Over mixing will make the muffins tough.)
3. Pour the batter into 6 cupcake molds, dividing it evenly. Then divide the blueberries evenly among the muffins and lightly press them into the batter so that they are at least partially submerged.
4. Place the molds in the air fryer and bake at 350°F for 16 minutes. Let cool before enjoying.

Nutrition:
Calories: 248 Fat: 3g Carbohydrates: 50g Fiber: 4g Proteins: 6g

15. Apple Pie Oat Bowls

Preparation time: 12 minutes   Cooking time: 6 minutes   Servings: 2

Ingredients:
- ⅔ cup rolled oats
- 1 apple, cored and diced
- 4 dates, pitted and diced
- ½ teaspoon ground cinnamon
- ¾ cup unsweetened plant-based milk

Directions:
1. In a heatproof cake pan or bowl, combine the oats, apple, dates, and cinnamon. Pour the plant-based milk over the top.
2. Bring the pan in the air fryer and bake at 350F for 6 minutes. Remove the pan and stir until well mixed. Bake for another 6 minutes until the apples are soft.
3. Stir again and let cool slightly before enjoying.

Nutrition:
Calories: 222 Fat: 3g Carbohydrates: 44g Fiber: 7g Proteins: 7g

16. Hash Browns

Preparation time: 12 minutes   **Cooking time:** 12 minutes   Servings: 4

Ingredients:
- 3 cups frozen shredded potatoes, thawed
- 2 tablespoons nutritional yeast
- 1 teaspoon No-Salt Spice Blend
- 1 tablespoon Aquafina
- 1 Cut 4 pieces of parchment paper, each about 12 inches long.

Directions:
1. In a medium bowl, mix the potatoes, nutritional yeast, spice blend, and Aquafina until well combined. Divide the mixture into 4 equal portions.
2. Place 1 portion onto the middle of a piece of parchment paper. Fold the sides of the paper together and then the top and bottom to create a rectangle about 3 by 5 inches. With the use of your hand, push down on the hash brown to flatten and spread it.
3. Unwrap the parchment paper and use a spatula to carefully transfer the hash brown to the air fryer basket or rack. Repeat step 3 with the remaining portions.
4. Fry the hash browns at 400F for 12 minutes, or until they are lightly browned and crispy. Be sure to flip the hash browns halfway through cooking. Enjoy the warmth.

Nutrition:
Calories: 92 Fat: 0g Carbohydrates: 20g Fiber: 3g Proteins: 3g

17. Apple-Cinnamon Breakfast Cookies

Preparation time: 5 Minutes   Cooking time: 9 Minutes   Servings: 15

Ingredients:

- 1 medium apple
- 1 cup oat flour
- 2 tablespoons pure maple syrup
- ¼ cup natural peanut butter
- ⅓ cup raisins
- ½ teaspoon ground cinnamon

Directions:
1. Using a grater or a julienne mandolin, carefully grate each side of the apple down to the core. Bring the grated apple in a medium bowl along with the oat flour, maple syrup, peanut butter, raisins and cinnamon. Mix until well combined.
2. Scoop out 2-tablespoon balls of dough onto parchment paper. Wet your hand to avoid sticking and flatten each cookie.
3. Bring the cookies from the parchment paper to the air fryer basket or rack and bake at 350F for 9 minutes, or until the edges of the cookies start to brown. Enjoy the warmth.

Nutrition:
Calories: 384 Fat: 14g Carbohydrates: 58g fiber: 6g Proteins: 11g

18. Cinnamon Rolls

Preparation time: 10 minutes　　Cooking time: 8 minutes　　Servings: 8

Ingredients:
- ½ (16-ounce) frozen pizza dough, thawed
- ⅓ cup Date Paste
- ¼ cup natural peanut butter
- ½ teaspoon ground cinnamon
- Nonstick cooking spray

Directions:
1. With a sheet of parchment paper, set out the pizza dough to about a 6-by-9-inch rectangle.
2. Spread the date paste and peanut butter evenly over the dough, covering it all the way to the edges. Then sprinkle the cinnamon evenly on top.
3. Roll the dough into a log. Set the log into 8 equal pieces, being careful not to compress the dough too much.
4. Place the pieces, spiral-side up, in your air fryer basket or on a flat tray. Let the dough rest and rise.
5. Lightly spray the rolls with cooking spray. Bake at 360F for 8 minutes, or until lightly browned. Serve warm.

Nutrition:
Calories: 270 Fat: 10g Carbohydrates: 39g Fiber: 3g Proteins: 9g

19. Tofu Scramble Brunch Bowls

Preparation time: 10 minutes　　Cooking time: 15 minutes　　Servings: 2

Ingredients:
- 1 medium russet potato, cut into fries or 1-inch cubes
- 1 bell pepper, seedless and cut into 1-inch strips
- ½ (14-ounce) block medium-firm tofu, drained and cubed
- 1 tablespoon nutritional yeast
- ½ teaspoon granulated garlic
- ½ teaspoon granulated onion
- ¼ teaspoon ground turmeric
- 1 tablespoon apple cider vinegar

Directions:
1. Place the potato and pepper strips in the air fryer basket or on the rack and fry at 400°F for 10 minutes.
2. Meanwhile, in a small pan, place the tofu, nutritional yeast, granulated garlic, granulated onion, turmeric and apple cider vinegar and stir gently to combine.
3. Add the pan to the air fryer, on a rack above the potatoes and peppers. Continue to fry at 400F for an additional 5 minutes, or until the potatoes are crispy and the tofu is heated through.
4. Detach the food from the air fryer and stir the tofu in the pan. Divide the potatoes and peppers evenly between 2 bowls. Then spoon half the tofu over each bowl. Serve warm.

Nutrition:
Calories: 267 Fat: 6g Carbohydrates: 42g Fiber: 4g Proteins: 15g

20. PB and J Power Tarts

Preparation time: 15 minutes   Cooking time: 8 minutes   Servings: 2

Ingredients:
- ¼ cup natural peanut butter
- 1 tablespoon coconut sugar
- 2 tablespoons unsweetened coconut yogurt
- ½ cup oat flour
- 2 tablespoons Blueberry Fruit Spread

Directions:
1. Cut 2 pieces of parchment paper, each 8 inches long. On one of the pieces of parchment paper, measure out and draw a 5-by-12-inch rectangle.
2. In a medium bowl, merge the peanut butter, coconut sugar, and coconut yogurt. Once they are combined, mix in the oat flour to form dough.
3. Place the dough on the blank piece of parchment paper and cover it with the other piece, with the rectangle facing you. Use a rolling pin to evenly set out the dough to fit in the rectangle. Carefully peel off the top piece of parchment paper.
4. Set the dough into 4 equal rectangles, each 3 by 5 inches. Place 1 tablespoon of the fruit spread on 2 of the rectangles and spread it out evenly. Carefully place the remaining 2 rectangles on top of the fruit spread and gently press on the edges with a fork.
5. Place the tarts in the air fryer basket or on the rack and bake at 350F for 8 minutes. Enjoy the warmth.

Nutrition:
Calories: 358 Fat: 19g Carbohydrates: 38g Fiber: 4g Proteins: 12g

21. Avocado Bagels

Preparation time: 25 minutes   Cooking time: 10 minutes   Servings: 2

Ingredients:
- ⅔ cup all-purpose flour
- ½ teaspoon active dry yeast
- ⅓ cup unsweetened coconut yogurt
- 8 cherry or grape tomatoes
- 1 ripe avocado
- 1 tablespoon freshly squeezed lemon juice
- 2 tablespoons finely chopped red onion
- Freshly ground black pepper

Directions:
1. In a bowl, merge the flour, yeast, and coconut yogurt. Knead into smooth dough.
2. Divide the dough into 2 equal balls. Roll each ball into a 9-inch-long rope. Then form a ring with each rope and press the ends together to connect them, creating 2 bagels.
3. Fill a medium bowl with hot (but not boiling) water. Soak the bagels in the water for 1 minute. Then shake off the excess water and move them to the air fryer basket or rack to rise for 15 minutes.
4. Bake at 400F for 5 minutes. Then flip the bagels over and add the tomatoes to the air fryer basket. Bake for an additional 5 minutes.
5. 5 Meanwhile, cut the avocado in half and carefully remove the pit. Scoop the avocado out into a small bowl and mash it with a fork. Mix in the lemon juice and red onion.
6. Let the bagels cool slightly before cutting them in half. Divide the avocado mixture among the 4 bagel halves. Top each bagel half with 2 baked tomatoes and season with pepper.

Nutrition:
Calories: 375 Fat: 16g Carbohydrates: 52g Fiber: 9g Proteins: 9g

22. Samosa Rolls

Preparation time: 15 minutes   Cooking time: 15 minutes   Servings: 8

Ingredients:
- ⅔ cup frozen peas, thawed
- 4 scallions, both white and green parts
- 2 cups grated sweet potato
- 2 tablespoons freshly squeezed lemon juice
- 1 teaspoon ground ginger
- 1 teaspoon curry powder
- ¼ cup chickpea flour
- 1 tablespoon tahini
- ⅓ cup water

- 8 (6-inch) rice paper wrappers

Directions:
1. In a medium bowl, combine the peas, scallions, sweet potato, lemon juice, ginger, curry powder, and chickpea flour. Set aside.
2. In a small bowl, merge the tahini and water until well combined. Pour the mixture onto a plate.
3. Dip both sides of a rice paper wrapper into the tahini mixture. When the wrapper starts to soften up, transfer it to another plate.
4. Spoon one-eighth of the filling (about ⅓ cups) onto the wrapper and wrap it up tightly, burrito style. Place the roll, seam-side down, in the air fryer basket or on the rack, and redo this process.
5. Bake at 350F for 15 minutes until the wrappers are lightly browned and crispy. Flip the rolls over halfway through cooking. Serve warm.

Nutrition:
Calories: 222 Fat: 6g Carbohydrates: 43g Fiber: 5g Proteins: 3g

23. Tofu-Spinach Scramble

Preparation time: 15 minutes   **Cooking time:** 15-16 minutes   Servings: 5

Ingredients:
- 1 (14-ounce) package water-packed extra-firm tofu
- 1 tsp. extra-virgin olive oil
- 1 small yellow onion, diced
- 3 teaspoons minced garlic (about 3 cloves)
- 3 large celery stalks, chopped
- 2 large carrots, peeled (optional) and chopped
- 1 teaspoon chili powder
- ½ teaspoon ground cumin
- ½ teaspoon ground turmeric
- ½ teaspoon salt (optional)
- ¼ teaspoon freshly ground black pepper
- 5 cups loosely packed spinach

Directions:
1. Drain the tofu by placing it, wrapped in a paper towel on a plate in the sink. Place a cutting board over the tofu, then set a heavy pot, can, or cookbook on the cutting board. Remove after 10 minutes. (Alternatively, use a tofu press).
2. In a medium bowl, crumble the tofu with your hands or a potato masher.
3. Heat the olive oil. Add the onion, garlic, celery, and carrots, and sauté for 5 minutes until the onion is softened.
4. Add the crumbled tofu, chili powder, cumin, turmeric, salt (if using), and pepper, and continue cooking for 7 to 8 more minutes, stirring frequently, until the tofu begins to brown.
5. Add the spinach and mix well. Cover and reduce the heat to medium. Steam the spinach for 3 minutes.
6. Divide evenly among 5 single-serving containers. Let cool before sealing the lids.

Nutrition:
Calories: 122 Fat: 15g Proteins: 14g Carbohydrates: 54g Fiber: 8g

24. Savory Pancakes

Preparation time: 10 minutes   Cooking time: 15 minutes   Servings: 4

Ingredients:
- 1 cup whole-wheat flour
- 1 teaspoon garlic salt
- 1 teaspoon onion powder
- ½ teaspoon baking soda
- ¼ teaspoon salt
- 1 cup lightly pressed, crumbled soft or firm tofu
- ½ cup unsweetened plant-based milk
- ¼ cup lemon juice
- 2 tablespoons extra-virgin olive oil
- ½ cup finely chopped mushrooms
- ½ cup finely chopped onion
- 2 cups tightly packed greens (arugula, spinach, or baby kale work great)

Directions:

1. Attach the flour, garlic salt, onion powder, baking soda, and salt. Mix well. In a blender, combine the tofu, plant-based milk, lemon juice, and olive oil. Purée at high speed for 30 seconds.
2. Spill the contents of the blender into the bowl of the dry ingredients and whisk until combined well. Fold in the mushrooms, onion, and greens.

Nutrition:
Calories: 132 Fat: 10g Proteins: 12g Carbohydrates: 44g Fiber: 9g

25. English Muffins with Tofu

Preparation time: 10 minutes   Cooking time: 15 minutes   Servings: 4

Ingredients:
- 2 tablespoons olive oil
- 16 ounces extra-firm tofu
- 1 tablespoon nutritional yeast
- ¼ teaspoon turmeric powder
- 2 handfuls fresh kale, chopped
- Kosher salt and ground black pepper, to flavor
- 4 English muffins, cut in half
- 4 tablespoons ketchup
- 4 slices vegan cheese

Directions:
1. Warmth the olive oil in a frying skillet over medium heat. When it's hot, add the tofu and sauté for 8 minutes, stirring occasionally to promote even cooking.
2. Add in the nutritional yeast, turmeric and kale and continue sautéing an additional 2 minutes or until the kale wilts. Season with salt and pepper to taste.
3. Meanwhile, toast the English muffins until crisp.
4. To assemble the sandwiches, spread the bottom halves of the English muffins with ketchup; top them with the tofu mixture and vegan cheese; place the bun topper on, close the sandwiches and serve warm.
5. Bon appétit!

Nutrition:
Calories: 150 Fat: 7.3g Fiber: 6.1g Carbohydrates: 18g Proteins: 3.7g

26. Multigrain Hot Cereal with Apricots

Preparation time: 30 minutes   Cooking time: 17 minutes   Servings: 2

Ingredients:
- ¼ cup long-grain brown rice
- 2 tablespoons rye
- 2 tablespoons millet
- 2 tablespoons wheat berries
- 2 tablespoons barley
- 6 dried apricots, chopped
- 2 cups water

Directions:
1. Clean the grains and soak them in water for 30 minutes until softened and drain.
2. In a saucepan, add the soaked grains, apricots, and 2 cups of water and stir to combine.
3. Cook for about 17 minutes over low heat, or until the liquid is absorbed, stirring periodically.
4. Allow to cool before serving.

Nutrition:
Calories: 242 Fat: 1.6g Carbohydrates: 50.5g Proteins: 6.5g Fiber: 6.1g

27. Cinnamon Pear Oatmeal

Preparation time: 10 minutes   Cooking time: 15 minutes   Servings: 22

Ingredients:
- 3 cups water
- 1 cup steel-cut oats
- 1 tbsp. cinnamon powder
- 1 cup pear, cored and peeled, cubed

Directions:
1. Take a pot and attach the water, oats, cinnamon, and pear and toss well. Bring it to parboil over medium heat.
2. Let it cook for 15 minutes and set into two bowls.
3. Enjoy!

Nutrition:
Calories: 365 Fat: 11g Carbohydrates: 48g Fiber: 9g

28. Hearty Pineapple Oatmeal

Preparation time: 10 minutes Cooking time: 4-8 hours Servings: 4

Ingredients:
- 1 cup steel-cut oats
- 4 cups unsweetened almond milk
- 2 medium apples, sliced
- 1 teaspoon coconut oil
- 1 teaspoon cinnamon
- ¼ teaspoon nutmeg
- 2 tablespoons maple syrup, unsweetened
- A drizzle of lemon juice

Directions:
1. Attach listed ingredients to a cooking pan and mix well. Cook on very low flame for 8 hours/or on high flame for 4 hours.
2. Gently stir. Attach your desired toppings.
3. Serve and enjoy!

Nutrition:
Calories: 332 Carbohydrates: 44.5g Proteins: 14.5g Fat: 9.25g

29. Cool Mushroom Munchies

Preparation time: 5 minutes. **Cooking time:** 10 minutes. Servings: 2

Ingredients:
- 4 Portobello mushroom caps
- 3 tablespoons coconut amines
- 2 tbsp. sesame oil
- 1 tbsp. fresh ginger, minced
- 1 small garlic clove, minced

Directions:
1. Set your broiler to low, keeping the rack 6 inches from the heating source. Rinse mushrooms under cold water and transfer them to a baking sheet (top side down).
2. Take a bowl and merge in sesame oil, garlic, coconut aminos, ginger and pour the mixture over the mushrooms tops.
3. Cook for 10 minutes. Serve and enjoy!

Nutrition:
Calories: 248 Fat: 3g Carbohydrates: 50g Fiber: 4g

30. Delightful Berry Quinoa Bowl

Preparation time: 5 minutes. **Cooking time:** 15 minutes. Servings: 4

Ingredients:
- 1 cup quinoa
- 2 cups of water
- 1 piece, 2-inch sized cinnamon stick
- 2-3 tablespoons of maple syrup

Flavorful Toppings
- ½ cup blueberries, raspberries or strawberries
- 2 tablespoons raisins
- 1 teaspoon lime
- ¼ teaspoon nutmeg, grated
- 3 tablespoons whipped coconut cream
- 2 tablespoon cashew nuts, chopped

Directions:
1. Take a metal strainer and pass your grain through them to strain them well. Rinse the grains under cold water thoroughly.
2. Take a medium-sized saucepan and pour in the water.
3. Add the strained grains and bring the whole mixture to a boil.
4. Add cinnamon sticks and cover the saucepan.
5. Lower the heat and let the mixture parboil for 15 minutes to allow the grain to absorb the liquid. Remove the heat and fluff up the mixture using a fork.
6. Add maple syrup if you want additional flavor. Also, if you are looking to make things a bit more interesting, just add any of the above-mentioned ingredients.

Nutrition:
Calories: 187 Carbohydrates: 33.7g Proteins: 8.45g Fat: 2.5g

31. Cinnamon-Banana French Toast

Preparation time: 5 minutes. Cooking time: 3 minutes. Servings: 3

Ingredients:
- ⅓ cup coconut milk
- ½ cup banana, mashed
- 2 tablespoons bean (chickpea flour)
- ½ teaspoon baking powder
- ½ teaspoon vanilla paste
- A pinch of sea salt
- 1 tablespoon agave syrup
- ½ teaspoon ground allspice
- A pinch of grated nutmeg
- 6 slices day-old sourdough bread
- 2 bananas, sliced
- 2 tablespoons brown sugar
- 1 teaspoon ground cinnamon

Directions:
1. To make the batter, thoroughly combine the coconut milk, mashed banana, bean, baking powder, vanilla, salt, agave syrup, allspice and nutmeg.
2. Set each slice of bread into the batter until well coated on all sides.
3. Preheat an electric griddle to medium heat and lightly oil it with a nonstick cooking spray.
4. Cook each slice of bread on the preheated griddle for about 3 minutes per side until golden brown.
5. Garnish the French toast with the bananas, brown sugar and cinnamon. Bon appétit!

Nutrition:
Calories: 222 Fat: 6g Carbohydrates: 43g Fiber: 5g Proteins: 3g

32. Frosty Hemp and Blackberry Smoothie Bowl

Preparation time: 5 minutes. Cooking time: 0 minutes. Servings: 2

Ingredients:
- 2 tablespoons hemp seeds
- ½ cup coconut milk
- 1 cup coconut yogurt
- 1 cup blackberries, frozen
- 2 small-sized bananas, frozen
- 4 tablespoons granola

Directions:
1. In your blender, mix all ingredients, trying to keep the liquids at the bottom of the blender to help it break up the fruits.
2. Divide your smoothie between serving bowls.
3. Garnish each bowl with granola and some extra frozen berries, if desired. Serve immediately!

Nutrition:
Calories: 219 Fat: 4.9g Carbohydrates: 38.0g Proteins: 7.2g Fiber: 6.0g

33. Chocolate and Walnut Steel-Cut Oats

Preparation time: 5 minutes Cooking time: 28 minutes Servings: 3

Ingredients:
- 2 cups oat milk
- ⅓ cup steel-cut oats
- 1 tablespoon coconut oil
- ¼ cup coconut sugar
- A pinch of grated nutmeg
- A pinch of flaky sea salt
- ¼ teaspoon cinnamon powder
- ¼ teaspoon vanilla extract
- 4 tablespoons cocoa powder
- ⅓ cup English walnut halves
- 4 tablespoons chocolate chips

Directions:
1. Bring the oat milk and oats to a boil over a moderately high heat. Then, turn the heat to low and add in the coconut oil, sugar and spices; let it simmer for about 25 minutes, stirring periodically.
2. Add in the cocoa powder and continue simmering for an additional 3 minutes.
3. Spoon the oatmeal into serving bowls. Top each bowl with the walnut halves and chocolate chips.
4. Bon appétit!

Nutrition:

Calories: 660 Fat: 19g Carbohydrates: 110g Fiber: 10g Proteins: 15g

34. Traditional Indian Roti

Preparation time: 5 minutes.   **Cooking time:** 10 minutes.   Servings: 5

Ingredients:
- 2 cups bread flour
- 1 teaspoon baking powder
- ½ teaspoon salt
- ¾ warm water
- 1 cup vegetable oil, for frying

Directions:
1. Thoroughly merge the flour, baking powder and salt in a mixing bowl. Gradually add in the water until the dough comes together.
2. Divide the dough into five balls; flatten each ball to create circles.
3. Heat the olive oil in a frying pan over a moderately high flame. Fry the first bread, turning it over to promote even cooking; fry it for about 10 minutes or until golden brown.
4. Repeat with the remaining dough. Transfer each roti to a paper towel-lined plate to drain the excess oil.
5. Bon appétit!

Nutrition:
Calories: 339.8 Fat: 19g Carbohydrates: 39g Proteins: 4.3g Fiber: 1g

35. Chocolate Chia Pudding

Preparation time: 5 minutes   Cooking time: 0 minutes   Servings: 4

Ingredients:
- 4 tablespoons unsweetened cocoa powder
- 4 tablespoons maple syrup
- 1 ⅔ cups coconut milk
- A pinch of grated nutmeg
- A pinch of ground cloves
- ½ teaspoon ground cinnamon
- ½ cup chia seeds

Directions:
1. Add the cocoa powder, maple syrup, milk and spices to a bowl and stir until everything is well incorporated.
2. Add in the chia seeds and stir again to combine well. Spoon the mixture into four jars, cover and place in your refrigerator overnight.
3. On the actual day, stir with a spoon and serve. Bon appétit!

Nutrition:
Calories: 222 Fat: 3g Carbohydrates: 44g Fiber: 7g

36. Easy Morning Polenta

Preparation time: 5 minutes   Cooking time: 18 minutes   Servings: 2

Ingredients:
- 2 cups vegetable broth
- ½ cup cornmeal
- ½ teaspoon sea salt
- ¼ tsp. ground black pepper, to taste
- ¼ teaspoon red pepper flakes, crushed
- 2 tablespoons olive oil

Directions:
1. In a medium saucepan, set the vegetable broth to boil over medium-high heat. Now, add in the cornmeal, whisking continuously to prevent lumps.
2. Set with salt, black pepper and red pepper.
3. Reduce the heat to a simmer. Continue to simmer, whisking periodically, for about 18 minutes, until the mixture has thickened.
4. Now, spill the olive oil into a saucepan and stir to combine well. Bon appétit!

Nutrition:
Calories: 365 Fat: 11g Carbohydrates: 48g Fiber: 9g

37. Mixed Berry and Almond Butter Swirl Bowl

Preparation time: 5 minutes   Cooking time: 0 minutes   Servings: 3

Ingredients:
- 1 ½ cups almond milk
- 2 small bananas
- 2 cups mixed berries, fresh or frozen
- 3 dates, pitted
- 3 scoops hemp protein powder
- 3 tablespoons smooth almond butter
- 2 tablespoons pepitas

Directions:
1. In your blender or food processor, mix the almond milk with the bananas, berries and dates.
2. Process until everything is well combined. Divide the smoothie between three bowls.
3. Top each smoothie bowl with almond butter and use a butter knife to swirl the almond butter into the top of each smoothie bowl.
4. Afterwards, garnish each smoothie bowl with pepitas, serve well-chilled and enjoy!

Nutrition:
Calories: 248 Fat: 3g Carbohydrates: 50g Fiber: 4g

38. Everyday Oats with Coconut and Strawberries

Preparation time: 5 minutes   Cooking time: 12 minutes   Servings: 2

Ingredients:
- ½ tablespoon coconut oil
- 1 cup rolled oats
- A pinch of flaky sea salt
- ⅛ teaspoon grated nutmeg
- ¼ teaspoon cardamom
- 1 tablespoon coconut sugar
- 1 cup coconut milk, sweetened
- 1 cup water
- 2 tablespoons coconut flakes
- 4 tablespoons fresh strawberries

Directions:
1. In a saucepan, dissolve the coconut oil over a moderate flame. Then, toast the oats for about 3 minutes, stirring continuously.
2. Add in the salt, nutmeg, cardamom, coconut sugar, milk and water; continue to cook for 12 minutes more or until cooked through.
3. Set the mixture into serving bowls, top with coconut flakes and fresh strawberries. Bon appétit!

Nutrition:
Calories: 466 Fat: 27g Carbohydrates: 29.4g Proteins: 26.6g

39. The Best Chocolate Granola Ever

Preparation time: 5 minutes   Cooking time: 60 minutes   Servings: 10

Ingredients:
- ½ cup coconut oil
- ½ cup agave syrup
- 1 teaspoon vanilla paste
- 3 cups rolled oats
- ½ cup hazelnuts, chopped
- ½ cup pumpkin seeds
- ½ teaspoon ground cardamom
- 1 teaspoon ground cinnamon
- ¼ teaspoon ground cloves
- 1 teaspoon Himalayan salt
- ½ cup dark chocolate, cut into cubes

Directions:
1. Begin by preheating your oven to 260 F: line two rimmed baking sheets with a piece of parchment paper.
2. Then, thoroughly combine the coconut oil, agave syrup and vanilla in a mixing bowl.
3. Gradually add in the oats, hazelnuts, pumpkin seeds and spices; toss to coat well. Set the mixture out onto the prepared baking sheets.
4. Bake in the middle of the oven, stirring halfway through the cooking time, for about 1 hour or until golden brown.
5. Stir in the dark chocolate and let your granola cool completely before storing. Store in an airtight container.
6. Bon appétit!

Nutrition:

Calories: 194 Carbohydrates: 43.3g Proteins: 3.4g Fat: 0.3g

40. Autumn Pumpkin Griddle Cakes

Preparation time: 5 minutes Cooking time: 6 minutes Servings: 4

Ingredients:
- ½ cup oat flour
- ½ cup whole-wheat white flour
- 1 teaspoon baking powder
- ¼ teaspoon Himalayan salt
- 1 teaspoon sugar
- ½ teaspoon ground allspice
- ½ teaspoon ground cinnamon
- ½ teaspoon crystalized ginger
- 1 teaspoon lemon juice, freshly squeezed
- ½ cup almond milk
- ½ cup pumpkin puree
- 2 tablespoons coconut oil

Directions:
1. In a mixing bowl, thoroughly merge the flour, baking powder, salt, sugar and spices. Gradually add in the lemon juice, milk and pumpkin puree.
2. Heat an electric griddle on medium and lightly slick it with the coconut oil.
3. Cook your cake for approximately 3 minutes until the bubbles form; flip it and cook on the other side for 3 minutes longer until browned on the underside.
4. Repeat with the remaining oil and batter. Serve dusted with cinnamon sugar, if desired. Bon appétit!

Nutrition:
Calories: 365 Fat: 11g Carbohydrates: 48g Fiber: 9g

41. Cinnamon Semolina Porridge

Preparation time: 5 minutes Cooking time: 30 minutes Servings: 3

Ingredients:
- 3 cups almond milk
- 3 tablespoons maple syrup
- 3 teaspoons coconut oil
- ¼ teaspoon kosher salt
- ½ teaspoon ground cinnamon
- 1 ¼ cups semolina

Directions:
1. In a saucepan, heat the almond milk, maple syrup, coconut oil, salt and cinnamon over a moderate flame.
2. Once hot, gradually stir in the semolina flour. Turn the heat to a simmer and continue cooking until the porridge reaches your preferred consistency.
3. Brush with your favorite toppings and serve warm. Bon appétit!

Nutrition:
Calories: 122 Fat: 15g Proteins: 14g Carbohydrates: 54g Fiber: 8g

42. Decadent Applesauce French Toast

Preparation time: 5 minutes Cooking time: 15 minutes Servings: 1

Ingredients:
- ¼ cup almond milk, sweetened
- 2 tablespoons applesauce, sweetened
- ½ teaspoon vanilla paste
- A pinch of salt
- A pinch of grated nutmeg
- ¼ teaspoon ground cloves
- ¼ teaspoon ground cinnamon
- 2 slices rustic day-old bread slices
- 1 tablespoon coconut oil
- 1 tablespoon maple syrup

Directions:
1. In a mixing bowl, thoroughly combine the almond milk, applesauce, vanilla, salt, nutmeg, cloves and cinnamon.
2. Set each slice of bread into the custard mixture until well coated on all sides.
3. Preheat the coconut oil in a frying pan over medium-high heat. Cook on each side, until golden brown.
4. Set the French toast with maple syrup and serve immediately. Bon appétit!

Nutrition:

Calories: 122 Fat: 15g Proteins: 14g Carbohydrates: 54g Fiber: 8g

43. Nutty Morning Bread Pudding

Preparation time: 5 minutes **Cooking time:** 2 hours 10 minutes Servings: 6

Ingredients:
- 1 ½ cups almond milk
- ½ cup maple syrup
- 2 tablespoons almond butter
- ½ teaspoon vanilla extract
- ½ teaspoon almond extract
- ½ teaspoon ground cinnamon
- ½ teaspoon ground cloves
- ⅓ teaspoon kosher salt
- ½ cup almonds, roughly chopped
- 4 cups day-old white bread, cubed

Directions:
1. In a mixing bowl, merge the almond milk, maple syrup, almond butter, vanilla extract, almond extract and spices.
2. Add the bread cubes to the custard mixture and stir to combine well. Fold in the almonds and allow it to rest for about 1 hour.
3. Then, spoon the mixture into a lightly oiled casserole dish.
4. Bake in the preheated oven at 350 F for about 1 hour or until the top is golden brown.
5. Place the bread pudding on a wire rack for 10 minutes before slicing and serving. Bon appétit!

Nutrition:
Calories: 278 Fat: 8.9g Carbohydrates: 41.9g Proteins: 12.0g Fiber: 11.4g

44. Moroccan Lentil and Raisin Salad

Preparation time: 5 minutes **Cooking time:** 15-17 minutes Servings: 4

Ingredients:
- 1 cup red lentils, rinsed
- 1 large carrot, julienned
- 1 Persian cucumber, thinly sliced
- 1 sweet onion, chopped
- ½ cup golden raisins
- ¼ cup fresh mint, snipped
- ¼ cup fresh basil, snipped
- ¼ cup extra-virgin olive oil
- ¼ cup lemon juice, freshly squeezed
- 1 teaspoon grated lemon peel
- ½ tsp. fresh ginger root, peeled and minced
- ½ teaspoon granulated garlic
- 1 teaspoon ground allspice
- Sea salt and ground black pepper

Directions:
1. In a large-sized saucepan, bring 3 cups of the water and 1 cup of the lentils to a boil.
2. Immediately turn the heat to a parboil and continue to cook your lentils for a further 15 to 17 minutes or until they've softened but are not mushy yet. Drain and let it cool completely.
3. Transfer the lentils to a salad bowl; add in the carrot, cucumber and sweet onion. Then, add the raisins, mint and basil to your salad.
4. In a small mixing dish, whisk the olive oil, lemon juice, lemon peel, ginger, granulated garlic, allspice, salt and black pepper.
5. Dress your salad and serve it well-chilled. Bon appétit!

Nutrition:
Calories: 523 Carbohydrates: 57.6g Proteins: 7.5g Fat: 37.6g

45. Pumpkin Oatmeal

Preparation time: 15 minutes Cooking time: 45 minutes Servings: 4

Ingredients:
- 2½ cups rolled oats
- 3 tablespoons chia seeds
- 1 teaspoon baking powder
- 1 teaspoon cinnamon
- ½ teaspoon cardamom
- ½ teaspoon salt
- 1¾ cups almond milk
- 1 (15-ounce) can pumpkin
- ⅓ cup maple syrup
- 1 tablespoon pure vanilla extract

Directions:
1. Preheat your oven to 350F.
2. Layer an 8x8-inch baking dish with wax paper.
3. Mix oats with salt, cardamom, cinnamon, baking powder, and chia seeds in a bowl.
4. Now, stir the rest of the oatmeal ingredients and mix it well until smooth.
5. Spread this batter in the baking dish and bake for 45 minutes.
6. Allow the oatmeal to cool and serve.

Nutrition:
Calories: 284 Fat: 7.9g Carbohydrates: 31g Fiber: 3.6g

46. Cauliflower Oatmeal

Preparation time: 5 minutes   Cooking time: 20 minutes   Servings: 2

Ingredients:

- 1 cup cauliflower rice
- ½ cup unsweetened almond milk
- ½ teaspoon cinnamon
- 1 tablespoon maple syrup
- ½ tablespoon peanut butter
- 1 strawberry, sliced

Directions:
1. Mix milk with cauliflower rice, honey and cinnamon in a saucepan.
2. Cook the rice mixture to a boil then reduce the heat to low.
3. Now cook the mixture for 10 minutes on a simmer.
4. Allow the oatmeal to cool, then garnish it with a strawberry.
5. Serve.

Nutrition:
Calories: 332 Carbohydrates: 44.5g Proteins: 14.5g Fat: 9.25g

47. Hemp Breakfast Cookies

Preparation time: 15 minutes   Cooking time: 15 minutes   Servings: 6

Ingredients:
- 3 cups almond flour
- 1 cup dried dates, pitted
- ½ cup hemp seeds
- 1 cup almond milk

Directions:
1. Mix almond milk with hemp seeds and dates in a bowl and leave for 1 hour.
2. Blend almond flour with the rest of the ingredients and milk mixture in a mixer until it makes a smooth dough.
3. Preheat your oven to 350F.
4. Set the dough into 9 portions and shape each into a cookie.
5. Place these cookies in a baking sheet, lined with wax paper.
6. Bake the cookies for 15 minutes in the oven and flip them once cooked halfway through.
7. Serve.

Nutrition:
Calories: 92 Fat: 0g Carbohydrates: 20g

48. Zucchini Oatmeal

Preparation time: 5 minutes   Cooking time: 4 minutes   Servings: 4

Ingredients:
- 2 cups rolled oats
- 6 tablespoons pea protein
- 2 teaspoons cinnamon
- 1 teaspoon nutmeg
- 2 ¼ cups almond milk
- 1 cup zucchini, grated
- ¼ cup maple syrup
- 1 teaspoon vanilla extract

Toppings
- Banana
- Nuts
- Seeds
- Sugar-free chocolate chips
- 1 teaspoon coconut oil

Directions:
1. Sauté oats with coconut oil in an Instant Pot for 2 minutes on Sauté mode.
2. Set in the rest of the ingredients, cover and seal its lid.
3. Cook for 2 minutes on high pressure.
4. When done, release all the pressure and remove the lid.
5. Allow the oatmeal to cool and garnish with desired toppings.
6. Serve.

Nutrition:
Calories: 150 Fat: 7.3g Fiber: 6.1g Carbohydrates: 18g Proteins: 3.7g

49. Peanut Butter Muffins

Preparation time: 15 minutes   Cooking time: 27 minutes   Servings: 6

Ingredients:
- ¾ cup oat flour
- ¼ cup coconut sugar
- 2 tablespoons pea protein powder
- 1 tablespoon baking powder
- 2 teaspoons baking soda
- 3 large bananas, mashed
- ½ cup peanut butter
- 2 tablespoons flaxseed
- ½ cup water
- ½ cup almond milk
- 1 teaspoon vanilla extract

Directions:
1. Preheat the oven to 350F and layer two muffin trays with cupcake liners.
2. Soak flaxseed with ½ cup water in a bowl for 5 minutes.
3. Mix mashed banana with milk, peanut butter and flaxseed mixture in a large bowl.
4. Now, stir it with the rest of the muffin ingredients and mix well evenly.
5. Divide the prepared batter into the muffin tray and bake for 27 minutes.
6. Allow the muffins to cool and serve.

Nutrition:
Calories: 395 Fat: 9.5g Carbohydrates: 34g Fiber: 0.4g

50. Chocolate Zucchini Bread

Preparation time: 15 minutes   Servings: 6
Cooking time: 55 minutes

Ingredients:
- 1¼ cup whole wheat flour
- ¾ cup coconut sugar
- ½ cup raw cacao powder
- 3 teaspoons baking powder
- 2 teaspoons baking soda
- 1 cup zucchini, shredded
- ½ cup almond milk
- ⅓ cup unsweetened applesauce
- ⅓ cup coconut oil, melted
- 2 teaspoons vanilla extract
- ⅔ cup sugar-free chocolate chip

Directions:
1. Preheat your oven to 350F and layer a 9-inch loaf pan with wax paper.
2. Dry the shredded zucchini and keep it aside.
3. Mix flour with baking soda, baking powder, cacao powder, coconut sugar and flour in a bowl.
4. Stir it with vanilla, applesauce, milk, and peanut butter, then mix until smooth.
5. Fold in sugar-free chocolate chips and zucchini shreds.
6. Spread this batter in the prepared loaf pan.
7. Bake this bread for 55 minutes in the oven.
8. Allow the bread to cool, then slice.
9. Serve.

Nutrition:
Calories: 375 Fat: 16g Carbohydrates: 52g Fiber: 9g Proteins: 9g

Lunch

51. French Onion Soup

Preparation time: 10 minutes.   **Cooking time:** 50 minutes.   Servings: 4

Ingredients:
- 4 medium onions, yellow or red, thinly sliced
- 3 tablespoons balsamic vinegar
- 3 cups vegetable stock
- 1 tablespoon dried thyme
- 3 dried bay leaves

Directions:
1. In a large nonstick saucepan, sauté the onions, stirring occasionally and adding 1 tablespoon of water at a time to prevent sticking, for about 25 minutes or until the onions are translucent and caramelized.
2. Add the vinegar and sauté for 5 more minutes, until the onions darken in color.
3. Attach the stock, 2 cups of water, the thyme, and bay leaves.
4. Cover and simmer for 20 minutes, until thickened.
5. Remove from the heat and discard the bay leaves.
6. Serve hot.

Serving Tip: For an authentic presentation, you can make bread tops for this soup. Use slices of a whole-grain baguette, top with a dollop of my Cheesy Sauce, and broil on high for 4 minutes.

Nutrition:
Calories: 68 Fat: 1g Proteins: 1g Carbohydrates: 15g Fiber: 2g

52. Lasagna Soup

Preparation time: 10 minutes.   **Cooking time:** 15 minutes.   Servings: 4

Ingredients:
- 2 cups mini whole-grain lasagna noodles
- 1 (26-ounce) can diced tomatoes
- 2 cups Mushroom Crumble
- 2½ tablespoons Italian seasoning

- 1 tablespoon garlic powder

Directions:
1. Set 5 cups of water to a boil and attach the pasta noodles. Boil for 6 minutes.
2. Set the heat to medium and attach the tomatoes, mushroom crumble, Italian seasoning, and garlic powder. Stir to combine.
3. Simmer for 5 minutes, until fragrant.
4. Detach from the heat and serve warm or allow cooling and refrigerating in an airtight container for up to 3 days.

Nutrition:
Calories: 244 Fat: 2g Proteins: 11g Carbohydrates: 50g Fiber: 10g

53. Black Bean and Mushroom Stew

Preparation time: 10 minutes. **Cooking time:** 20 minutes. Servings: 5

Ingredients:
- 7 cups sliced mushrooms (about 1 pound)
- 3 cups vegetable stock
- 1 (19-ounce) can black beans (about 2 cups cooked), rinsed and drained
- 3 tablespoons tomato paste
- 3 tablespoons Savory Spice

Directions:
1. In a nonstick saucepan over medium-high heat, sauté the mushrooms for 10 minutes, until soft and brown. Stir often to avoid sticking. Attach the stock, 1 tablespoon at a time, if needed to prevent sticking.
2. Attach the beans to the pan, along with the tomato paste and savory spice. Stir to combine.
3. Set to a boil over high heat, set the heat to low, cover, and simmer for 8 minutes. Stir occasionally.
4. Serve hot.

Nutrition:
Calories: 181 Fat: 1g Proteins: 14g Carbohydrates: 32g Fiber: 10g

54. Spicy Peanut Ramen

Preparation time: 5 minutes. **Cooking time:** 10 minutes. Servings: 4

Ingredients:
- 4 servings brown rice ramen noodles
- ½ cup Peanut Sauce
- 1 tablespoon Shichimi Togarashi Spice Mix
- 1 cup cooked edamame beans
- ½ cup chopped scallions

Directions:
1. Cook the noodles.
2. Meanwhile, in a nonstick pan, combine the peanut sauce, spice mix, beans, and ½ cup of water. Set the heat to medium and stew for 5 minutes, stirring occasionally, until warmed.
3. Drain the noodles and divide among 4 bowls.
4. Top with the warmed peanut sauce and edamame. Garnish with the scallions.
5. Serve immediately.

Nutrition:
Calories: 333 Fat: 9g Proteins: 13g Carbohydrates: 53g Fiber: 5g

55. Creamy Mushroom Soup

Preparation time: 10 minutes. **Cooking time:** 20 minutes. Servings: 4

Ingredients:
- 5 cups sliced mushrooms
- 5 garlic cloves, minced
- 1½ cups vegetable stock
- 1½ cups unsweetened plant-based milk
- 1 tablespoon dried thyme

Directions:

1. Warmth a deep nonstick pan over medium-high heat and sauté the mushrooms and garlic for 10 minutes or until the mushrooms are soft. Attach ¼ cup of water if the pan gets too dry.
2. Mix in the stock, plant-based milk, and thyme.
3. Set the heat to low and stew for 8 minutes, stirring occasionally, until the soup thickens.
4. Serve warm.

Nutrition:
Calories: 46 Fat: 1g Proteins: 3g Carbohydrates: 7g Fiber: 1g

56. Potato Harvest Stew

Preparation time: 10 minutes. **Cooking time:** 15 minutes. Servings: 5

Ingredients:
- 3 cups chopped, unpeeled yellow potatoes
- 1 cup sliced carrots
- 1 small yellow onion, diced
- 3 tablespoons tomato paste
- 1½ tablespoons poultry seasoning

Directions:
1. In a large stockpot, bring the potatoes and carrots to boil in 6 cups of water. Boil for 8 minutes.
2. Meanwhile, in a nonstick pan, sauté the onion.
3. Reserving 3 cups of the boiling water drains the potatoes and carrots.
4. In the stockpot, combine the reserved cooking water, tomato paste, and poultry seasoning. Stir to combine. Set to a boil over high heat and then reduce the heat to low.
5. Add the potatoes, carrots, and onion. Remove from the heat.
6. Serve warm.

Nutrition:
Calories: 114 Fat: 1g Proteins: 3g Carbohydrates: 26g Fiber: 4g

57. Quick Black Bean Chili

Preparation time: 5 minutes. **Cooking time:** 20 minutes. Servings: 5

Ingredients:
- 1 (15-ounce) can diced tomatoes
- 1 (19-ounce) can black beans, rinsed and washed
- 1½ cups tomato sauce
- 2 cups Mushroom Crumble
- 3 tablespoons Chipotle Spice

Directions:
1. In a pot with a lid, combine the tomatoes, black beans, tomato sauce, mushroom crumble, and chipotle spice. Stir.
2. Set to a boil over high heat and then set the heat to low. Cover and simmer, stirring occasionally, until fragrant, about 20 minutes.
3. Serve warm or allow cooling.

Nutrition:
Calories: 199 Fat: 1g Proteins: 13g Carbohydrates: 37g Fiber: 13g

58. Sweet Potato and Peanut Stew

Preparation time: 15 minutes. **Cooking time:** 30 minutes. Servings: 4

Ingredients:
- 2 onions, diced
- 2 tablespoons extra-virgin olive oil or coconut oil
- 2 large sweet potatoes, peeled and chopped
- ⅓ cup chunky peanut butter
- 1 teaspoon smoked paprika
- ¼ tsp. red pepper flakes
- 2 cups water or unsalted vegetable broth
- ¼ teaspoon salt
- 2 cups finely chopped fresh spinach or kale
- Freshly ground black pepper

Directions:
1. On your electric pressure cooker, select Sauté. Add the onions and olive oil, and then cook for 4-5 minutes, stirring occasionally, until the onion has softened. Stir in the sweet potatoes, peanut butter,

paprika, chili flakes, water and salt. Stir to mix the peanut butter with the water a little, but don't worry too much as it will melt when heated. Cancel Sauté.
2. High pressure for 6 minutes, close and lock the lid and make sure the pressure valve is sealed and set the time to 6 minutes.
3. Releasing the pressure. At the end of the cooking time, quickly release the pressure. Once all pressure has been released, carefully unlock and remove the lid. Incorporate the spinach to wilt. Set and season with more salt and pepper.

Nutrition:
Calories: 350 Proteins: 10g Fat: 18g Carbohydrates: 16g Fiber: 8g

59. Split Pea Soup

Preparation time: 10 minutes.   **Cooking time:** 30 minutes.   Servings: 6
Ingredients:
- 3 or 4 carrots, scrubbed or peeled and chopped
- 1 large yellow onion, chopped
- 1 cup dried split green peas
- 3 cups water or unsalted vegetable broth
- 1 tablespoon tamari or soy sauce
- 2 to 3 teaspoons dried thyme or 1 teaspoon ground thyme
- 1 teaspoon onion powder
- ½ teaspoon garlic powder
- Pinch freshly ground black pepper
- ¼ cup chopped sun-dried tomatoes or chopped pitted black olives
- Salt

Directions:
1. 1. In the electric pressure cooker, combine the carrots, onion, split peas, water, tamari, thyme, onion powder, garlic powder and pepper.
2. High pressure for 10 minutes. Secure and lock the lid and make sure the pressure valve is sealed, then select High pressure and set the time to 10 minutes.
3. Relief of pressure. Once the cooking time is done, let the pressure naturally release for about 20 minutes. Once all pressure is released, carefully unlock and remove the lid. Let it cool then blend the soup: use an immersion blender directly into the pot.

Nutrition:
Calories: 182 Proteins: 12g Fat: 1g Carbohydrates: 26g Fiber: 12

60. Sour Soup

Preparation time: 5 minutes   **Cooking time:** 20 minutes   Servings: 4
Ingredients:
- 2 tablespoons dried wood ears
- 3.5ounces bamboo shoots, sliced into thin strips
- 1 medium carrot, peeled, sliced into thin strips
- 5 dried shiitake mushrooms
- 1 tablespoon grated ginger
- 1 teaspoon minced garlic
- 1 teaspoon ground black pepper
- 1 teaspoon salt
- ¼ cup soy sauce
- 1 teaspoon sugar
- ½ cup rice vinegar
- 4 cups vegetable stock
- 1 ½ cup water, boiling
- 7.5ounces tofu, extra-firm, drained
- 1 tablespoon green onion tops, chopped
- ¼ cup water, at room temperature
- 2 tablespoons cornstarch
- 1 teaspoon sesame oil

Directions:
1. Take a small bowl, put some wooden ears in it, then pour the boiling water until it is covered and let it rest for 30 minutes.
2. In the meantime, take another bowl, put the mushrooms in it, pour 1 ½ cups of water and let the mushrooms rest for 30 minutes.
3. After 30 minutes, drain the ears of wood, rinse them well and cut them into slices, remove and discard the hard pieces.

4. Similarly, drain the mushrooms, reserving their soaking liquid and slice the mushrooms, removing and discarding their stems.
5. Take a large pot, put it on medium-high heat, add the whole Shopping List: including the reserved mushroom liquid, leave the last five Shopping List: mix well and bring to a boil.
6. Then bring the heat to medium and simmer the soup for 10 minutes until cooked.
7. Meanwhile, put the cornstarch in a bowl, add the room temperature water and mix well until smooth.
8. Cut the tofu into 1-inch pieces, add it to the hot soup along with the cornstarch mixture, and continue to simmer the soup until it reaches the desired thickness.
9. Drizzle with sesame oil, spread soup into bowls, garnish with green onions and serve.

Nutrition:
Calories: 152 Fat: 2g Carbohydrates: 35g Proteins: 4g Fiber: 8g

61. Roasted Tomato Soup

Preparation time: 10 minutes. **Cooking time:** 50 minutes. Servings: 4

Ingredients:
- 2 pounds ripe tomatoes, cored and halved
- 2 large garlic cloves, crushed
- 3 tablespoons extra-virgin olive oil
- 1 tablespoon balsamic vinegar
- Salt and freshly ground black pepper
- ½ cup chopped red onion
- 2 cups light vegetable broth or store-bought, or water
- ½ cup lightly packed fresh basil leaves

Directions:
1. Preheat the oven to 450F. In a large bowl, merge the tomatoes, garlic, 2 tablespoons of oil, vinegar, salt and pepper. Spread the tomato mixture into a 9 x 13-inch pan and roast until the tomatoes begin to brown for about 30 minutes. Remove from the oven and set aside.
2. In a large saucepan, warmth the remaining tablespoon of oil over medium heat. Attach the onion, cover and cook until very soft for about 10 minutes, stirring occasionally. Add the roasted tomatoes and stock, and then bring to a boil. Set the heat and simmer, uncovered, for 10 minutes. Remove from the heat, add the basil and season with salt and pepper. Merge the soup in the pot with an immersion blender or in a blender or food processor, as much as needed, and return to the pot. Reheat over medium heat if needed. To serve this cold soup, refrigerate it for at least 1 hour before serving.

Nutrition:
Calories: 222 Fat: 6g Carbohydrates: 43g Fiber: 5g Proteins: 3g

62. Butternut Squash

Preparation time: 10 minutes **Cooking time:** 35 minutes Servings: 6

Ingredients:
- 1 cup diced parsnips
- 2 cups diced sweet potato
- 1 large sweet onion, peeled, diced
- 1 ½ cups diced carrots
- 4 cups diced butternut squash
- 2 teaspoons minced garlic
- ¼ teaspoon ground ginger
- ¼ teaspoon ground black pepper
- ½ teaspoon of sea salt
- ¼ teaspoon ground allspice
- 1 teaspoon poultry seasoning
- 1 teaspoon pumpkin pie spice
- ¼ teaspoon ground cinnamon
- 32 ounces vegetable stock
- 14 ounces coconut milk, unsweetened

Directions:
1. Take a large Dutch oven, put it over medium heat, add the onions, and drizzle with 2 tablespoons of water and cook for 5 minutes until softened, sprinkling with more 2 tablespoons at a time as needed.
2. Then attach the garlic, cook for another minute, bring the heat to high, add the remaining shopping list: set aside milk, salt and black pepper and bring the soup to a boil.
3. Then change the heat to medium-low and simmer for 20 minutes until the vegetables are tender.

4. When done, blend the soup using a hand blender, then stir in the coconut milk, set with salt and pepper and cook.
5. Serve immediately.

Nutrition:
Calories: 188.4 Fat: 7.7g Carbohydrates: 29.3g Proteins: 3.7g Fiber: 8.2g

63. Wonton Soup

Preparation time: 15 minutes **Cooking time:** 10 minutes Servings: 4

Ingredients:
For the Soup:
- 4 cups vegetable broth
- 2 green onions, chopped

For the Wontons Filling:
- 1 cup chopped mushrooms
- ¼ cup walnuts, chopped
- 1 green onion, chopped
- ½ inch of ginger, grated
- ½ teaspoon minced garlic
- 1 tablespoon rice vinegar
- 2 teaspoons soy sauce
- 1 teaspoon brown sugar
- 20 Vegan Wonton Wrappers

Directions:
1. Prepare the filling of the wontons and for this, take a bowl, and put the whole shopping list: in it, except the paper, and mix until well blended.
2. Place a wonton wrapper on the workspace, place 1 teaspoon of the prepared filling in the center, then brush some water around the edges, fold into a crescent shape, and seal the wraps by pinching the edges.
3. Take a large pot, put it on medium-high heat, add the broth and bring it to a boil.
4. Then pour in the prepared wontons, one at a time, and boil for 5 minutes.
5. When cooked, garnish the soup with green onions and serve.

Nutrition:
Calories: 196.9 Fat: 4g Carbohydrates: 31g Proteins: 6.6g Fiber: 2.4g

64. Potato and Kale Soup

Preparation time: 5 minutes **Cooking time:** 15 minutes Servings: 2

Ingredients:
- 1 small white onion, peeled, chopped
- 2 ½ cups cubed potatoes
- 2 cups leek, cut into rings
- ½ cup chopped carrots
- ½ cup chopped celery
- ½ teaspoon minced garlic
- ⅔ teaspoon salt
- ⅓ teaspoon ground black pepper
- 1 tablespoon olive oil
- 3 ½ cups vegetable broth
- 1 cup kale, cut into stripes
- Croutons, for serving

Directions:
1. Take a large pot, put it on medium heat, add the oil and, when it is hot, attach the onion and cook for 2 minutes until it is sautéed.
2. Set the garlic, cook for another minute, then add all the vegetables and continue cooking for 3 minutes.
3. Pour in the broth, cook for 15 minutes, then add the kale and cook for 2 minutes until tender.
4. Flavor the soup with salt and black pepper, blend using a hand blender until smooth, then top with croutons and serve.

Nutrition:
Calories: 337 Fat: 7g Carbohydrates: 62g Proteins: 10g Fiber: 8g

65. Ramen Soup

Preparation time: 10 minutes **Cooking time:** 20 minutes Servings: 2

Ingredients:
For the Mushrooms and Tofu:

- 2 cups sliced shiitake mushrooms
- 6 ounces tofu, extra-firm, drained, sliced

For the Noodle Soup:
- 2 packs of dried ramen noodles
- 1 medium carrot, peeled, grated
- 1 inch of ginger, grated
- 1 teaspoon minced garlic

For Garnish:
- Sesame seeds as needed
- Soy sauce as needed
- 1 tablespoon olive oil
- 1 tablespoon soy sauce
- ¾ cup baby spinach leaves
- 1 tablespoon olive oil
- 6 cups vegetable broth
- Sriracha sauce as needed

Directions:
1. Prepare the mushrooms and tofu and for this, put the tofu pieces in a plastic bag, add the soy sauce, seal the bag and turn it upside down until the tofu is coated.
2. Take a skillet, set it over medium heat, add the oil and, when hot, add the tofu slices and cook for 5-10 minutes until crisp and golden on all sides, turning often and when cooked., set aside until needed.
3. Attach the mushrooms to the pan, cook for 8 minutes until golden brown, pour the soy sauce from the tofu pieces and stir until coated.
4. In the meantime, prepare the noodle soup and for this, take a pot, put it on medium-high heat, attach the oil and when it is hot add the garlic and ginger and cook for 1 minute until not it is fragrant.
5. Then spill in the broth, bring the mixture to a boil, add the noodles and cook until tender.
6. Then mix the spinach into the noodle soup, remove the pot from the heat and distribute evenly between bowls.
7. Add the mushrooms and tofu along with the garnish and then serve.

Nutrition:
Calories: 647 Fat: 12g Carbohydrates: 106g Proteins: 28g Fiber: 6g

66. Vegetable and Barley Stew

Preparation time: 15 minutes **Cooking time:** 20 minutes Servings: 6

Ingredients:
- 2 or 3 parsnips, peeled and chopped
- 2 cups chopped peeled sweet potato, russet potato, winter squash, or pumpkin
- 1 large yellow onion, chopped
- 1 cup pearl barley
- 1 (28-ounce) can diced tomatoes
- 4 cups water or unsalted vegetable broth
- 2 to 3 teaspoons dried mixed herbs or 1 teaspoon dried basil plus 1 teaspoon dried oregano
- Salt
- Freshly ground black pepper

Directions:
1. In your electric pressure cooker, combine the parsnips, sweet potato, onion, and barley, tomatoes with their juice, water, and herbs.
2. High pressure for 20 minutes. Secure the lid, then select High pressure and set the time to 20 minutes.
3. Pressure release. Once the cooking time is finished, quickly release the pressure. Once all pressure has been released, carefully unlock and remove the lid. Taste and season with salt and pepper.

Nutrition:
Calories: 300 Proteins: 9g Fat: 2g Carbohydrates: 16g Fiber: 14g

67. Vegan Pho

Preparation time: 5 minutes **Cooking time:** 15 minutes Servings: 6

Ingredients:
- 1 package of wide rice noodles, cooked
- 1 medium white onion, peeled, quartered
- 2 teaspoons minced garlic
- 1 inch of ginger, sliced into coins
- 8 cups vegetable broth
- 3 whole cloves
- 2 tablespoons soy sauce
- 3 whole star anise

- 1 cinnamon stick

For Toppings:
- Basil as needed for topping
- Chopped green onions as needed for topping
- 3 cups of water
- Mung beans as needed for topping
- Hot sauce as needed for topping
- Lime wedges for serving

Directions:
1. Take a large pot, put it on medium-high heat, add the whole Shopping List: for the soup, except the soy sauce and broth, and bring to a boil.
2. Then change the heat to medium-low, simmer the soup for 30 minutes and then add the soy sauce.
3. When finished, spread the cooked noodles into bowls, add the soup, then garnish and serve.

Nutrition:
Calories: 31 Fat: 0g Carbohydrates: 7g Proteins: 0g Fiber: 2g

68. Garden Vegetable Stew

Preparation time: 6 minutes **Cooking time:** 60 minutes Servings: 4

Ingredients:
- 2 tablespoons extra-virgin olive oil
- 1 medium red onion, chopped
- 1 medium carrot
- ½ cup dry white wine
- 3 medium new potatoes, unpeeled and cut into 1-inch pieces
- 1 medium red bell pepper
- 1½ cups vegetable broth
- 2 medium zucchinis, trimmed, halved lengthwise, and cut into ½-inch slices
- 1 medium yellow summer squash, trimmed, halved lengthwise, and cut into ½-inch slices
- 1 pound ripe plum tomatoes, chopped
- Salt and freshly ground black pepper
- 2 cups fresh corn kernels
- 1 cup fresh peas
- ¼ cup fresh basil
- ¼ cup chopped fresh parsley
- 1 tbsp. minced fresh savory or 1 teaspoon dried

Directions:
1. In a large saucepan, warmth the oil over medium heat. Attach the onion and carrot, cover and cook until softened for 7 minutes. Attach the wine and cook, uncovered, for 5 minutes. Stir in the potatoes, pepper and broth, then bring to a boil. Lower the heat to medium and stew for 15 minutes.
2. Add the courgette, yellow squash and tomatoes. Flavor with salt and black pepper, cover and simmer until vegetables are tender for 20-30 minutes.
3. Finish and serve
4. Mix the corn, peas, basil, parsley and savory. Taste, adjusting the seasonings if necessary. Stew to mix the flavors for about 10 more minutes. Serve immediately.

Nutrition:
Calories: 166 Fat: 8g Carbohydrates: 24g Fiber: 6.5g Proteins: 9g

69. Moroccan Vegetable Stew

Preparation time: 5 minutes **Cooking time:** 35 minutes Servings: 4

Ingredients:
- 1 tablespoon extra-virgin olive oil
- 2 medium yellow onions, chopped
- 2 medium carrots
- ½ teaspoon ground cumin
- ½ teaspoon ground cinnamon or allspice
- ½ teaspoon ground ginger
- ½ teaspoon sweet or smoked paprika
- ½ teaspoon saffron or turmeric
- 1 (14.5-ounce) can diced tomatoes, undrained
- 8 ounces green beans
- 2 cups peeled, seeded, and diced winter squash
- 1 large russet or other baking potato, peeled and cut into ½-inch dice
- 1½ cups vegetable broth
- 1½ cups cooked or 1 can chickpeas, drained and rinsed
- ¾ cup frozen peas
- ½ cup pitted dried plums (prunes)

- 1 teaspoon lemon zest
- Salt and freshly ground black pepper
- ½ cup pitted green olives
- 1 tablespoon minced fresh cilantro or parsley, for garnish
- ½ cup toasted slivered almonds, for garnish

Directions:
1. In a large saucepan, warmth the oil over medium heat. Attach the onions and carrots, cover and cook for 5 minutes. Incorporate the cumin, cinnamon, ginger, paprika and saffron. Cook uncovered and mix for 30 seconds. Add the tomatoes, green beans, squash, potato and broth and bring to a boil. Lower the heat, secure and simmer until the vegetables are tender for about 20 minutes.
2. Finish and serve
3. Add the chickpeas, peas, prunes and lemon zest. Season with salt and pepper. Incorporate the olives and simmer, uncovered, until the flavors have blended for about 10 minutes. Sprinkle it with cilantro and almonds, and then serve immediately.

Nutrition:
Calories: 139 Fat: 1.4g Carbohydrates: 28g Fiber: 11g Proteins: 5g

70. Matzo Ball Soup

Preparation time: 5 minutes **Cooking time:** 45 minutes Servings: 4

Ingredients:
- 1 tablespoon extra-virgin olive oil
- 1 small onion, finely chopped
- 1 medium carrot, chopped
- 1 celery rib, chopped
- 3 green onions, chopped
- 6 cups vegetable broth, homemade or store-bought, or water
- 2 tablespoons minced fresh parsley
- 1 teaspoon fresh or dried dill weed
- ½ teaspoon salt, or more if needed
- ¼ teaspoon freshly ground black pepper
- Matzo Balls (recipe follows)

Directions:
1. In a large saucepan, set the oil over medium heat. Add the onion, carrot and celery. Secure and cook until softened for about 5 minutes. Add the green onions and cook for 3 minutes more. Incorporate the broth, parsley, dill, salt and pepper. Set to a boil, and then lower the heat to low and simmer, uncovered, until the vegetables are tender for about 30 minutes.
2. Finish and serve
3. When ready to serve, place three matzo balls in each bowl and pour the soup over them. Serve immediately.

Nutrition:
Calories: 420 Fat: 15.2g Carbohydrates: 64.3g Proteins: 11.6g

71. White Bean and Broccoli Salad

Preparation time: 10 minutes **Cooking time:** 15 minutes Servings: 4-6

Ingredients:
- 1 pound Yukon Gold potatoes, peel off and cut into 1-inch chunks
- 3 cups broccoli florets
- 1½ cups cooked or 15.5-ounce can cannellini or other white beans, drained and rinsed
- ¼ cup kalamata olives
- ½ cup walnut pieces
- 2 garlic cloves, finely minced
- ½ cup chopped fresh parsley
- ¼ cup walnut oil
- ¼ cup extra-virgin olive oil
- ¼ cup white wine vinegar
- ½ teaspoon salt (optional)
- ¼ teaspoon crushed red pepper

Directions:
1. Steam the potatoes until almost tender for about 10 minutes. Steam the broccoli until tender for about 5 minutes. Drain the potatoes and broccoli and put them in a large bowl. Add the beans, olives and ¼ cup of walnuts and set aside.

2. In a blender or food processor, merge the remaining ¼ cup of walnuts with the garlic and blend until well-chopped. Add the parsley, walnut oil, olive oil, vinegar, salt, sugar and chopped chili and blend until smooth. Spill the dressing over the salad, stirring gently to combine, and then serve.

Nutrition:
Calories: 294 Fat: 6g Carbohydrates: 19.5g Fiber: 12g Proteins: 22.5g

72. Chinese Black Bean Chili

Preparation time: 15 minutes   Cooking time: 0 minutes   Servings: 4

Ingredients:
- 1 tablespoon extra-virgin olive oil
- 1 medium yellow onion, finely chopped
- 2 medium carrots, finely chopped
- 1 teaspoon grated fresh ginger
- 2 tablespoons chili powder
- 1 teaspoon brown sugar
- 1 (28-ounce) can diced tomatoes, undrained
- ½ cup Chinese black bean sauce
- ¾ cup water
- ½ cans black beans, drained and rinsed
- Salt and freshly ground black pepper
- 2 tablespoons minced green onion, for garnish

Directions:
1. In a large saucepan, set the oil over medium heat. Add the onion and carrot. Cover and cook until softened for about 10 minutes.
2. Stir in the ginger, chili powder and sugar. Add the tomatoes, black bean sauce and water. Incorporate the black beans and season with salt and pepper.
3. Set to a boil, and then lower the heat to medium and simmer, covered, until the vegetables are tender for about 30 minutes.
4. Simmer for about 10 minutes more. Serve immediately garnished with green onion.

Nutrition:
Calories: 302 Fat: 22g Carbohydrates: 5g Proteins: 34g

73. Coconut Rice

Preparation time: 10 minutes   **Cooking time:** 25 minutes   Servings: 7

Ingredients:
- 2 ½ cups white rice
- ⅛ teaspoon salt
- 40 ounces coconut milk, unsweetened

Directions:
1. Take a large saucepan; put it on medium heat, add the whole Shopping List: inside and mix until combined.
2. Set the mixture to a boil, then bring the heat to medium-low and simmer the rice for 25 minutes until tender and all liquid is absorbed.
3. Serve immediately.

Nutrition:
Calories: 535 Fat: 33.2g Carbohydrates: 57g Proteins: 8.1g Fiber: 2.1g

74. Baked Beans

Preparation time: 5 minutes   **Cooking time:** 45 minutes   Servings: 4

Ingredients:
- 1 tablespoon extra-virgin olive oil
- 1 medium yellow onion, minced
- 3 garlic cloves, minced
- 1 (14.5-ounce) can crushed tomatoes
- ½ cup pure maple syrup
- 2 tablespoons blackstrap molasses
- 1 tablespoon soy sauce
- 1½ teaspoons dry mustard
- ¼ teaspoon ground cayenne
- Salt and freshly ground black pepper
- 3 cups cooked Great Northern beans

Directions:
1. Preheat the oven to 350F.
2. Lightly grease a 2-quart saucepan and set aside.

3. In a large saucepan, warmth the oil over medium heat. Add the onion and garlic. Secure and cook until softened for about 5 minutes.
4. Stir in the tomatoes, maple syrup, molasses, soy sauce, mustard, and cayenne pepper and set to a boil.
5. Set the heat to low and stew, unsealed, until slightly reduced for about 10 minutes. Season with salt and pepper.
6. Put the beans in the prepared saucepan. Add the sauce, stirring to mix and coat the beans. Cover and cook until hot and bubbly for about 30 minutes. Serve immediately

Nutrition:
Calories: 398 Carbohydrates: 55.6g Proteins: 17.8g Fat: 11.8g

75. Lemony Quinoa

Preparation time: 10 minutes   Cooking time: 0 minute   Servings: 6

Ingredients:
- 1 cup quinoa, cooked
- ¼ of medium red onion, peeled, chopped
- 1 bunch of parsley, chopped
- 2 stalks of celery, chopped
- ¼ teaspoon of sea salt
- ¼ teaspoon cayenne pepper
- ½ teaspoon ground cumin
- ¼ cup lemon juice
- ¼ cup pine nuts, toasted

Directions:
1. Take a large bowl, place all the Shopping List: in it, and stir until combined.
2. Serve straight away.

Nutrition:
Calories: 147 Fat: 4.8g Carbohydrates: 21.4g Proteins: 6g Fiber: 3g

76. Vegan Curried Rice

Preparation time: 5 minutes   **Cooking time:** 25 minutes   Servings: 4

Ingredients:
- 1 cup white rice
- 1 tablespoon minced garlic
- 1 tablespoon ground curry powder
- ⅓ teaspoon ground black pepper
- 1 tablespoon red chili powder
- 1 tablespoon ground cumin
- 2 tablespoons olive oil
- 1 tablespoon soy sauce
- 1 cup vegetable broth

Directions:
1. Take a saucepan, put it on low heat, add the oil and when it is hot attach the garlic and cook for 3 minutes.
2. Then add all the spices, cook for 1 minute until fragrant, pour in the broth and bring the heat to a high level.
3. Stir in the soy sauce, bring the mixture to a boil, add the rice, stir until combined, then turn the heat to low and simmer for 20 minutes until the rice is tender and all the liquid is absorbed.
4. Serve immediately.

Nutrition:
Calories: 262 Fat: 8g Carbohydrates: 43g Proteins: 5g Fiber: 2g

77. Spicy Cabbage Salad

Preparation time: 5 minutes   Cooking time: 5 minutes   Servings: 4

Ingredients:
- 1 head Napa cabbage
- 1 cup carrots
- ½ cup green onions
- 1 bell pepper
- ½ cup cilantro
- 1 jalapeño chili pepper
- ½ cup sunflower seeds
- ½ cup almond butter
- ¼ cup canned coconut milk
- ¼ cup apple cider vinegar
- ¼ cup onion
- 2 tbsp. white miso paste
- 2 tbsp. maple syrup
- 1 tbsp. red curry paste

- 3 garlic cloves
- ½-inch piece ginger

Directions:
1. Cut the end of the cabbage, halve and core it, then cut thinly. Shred carrots thinly slice green onions and pepper, chop cilantro and jalapeño. Combine all in a large bowl with sunflower seeds. Set aside.
2. Roughly chop onion.
3. Make the sauce by blending the almond butter, coconut milk, vinegar, onion, miso, maple syrup, curry paste, garlic, and ginger. Blend until smooth and mixed. If needed, attach water to thin it out.
4. Pour the dressing over the veggie mix and toss to coat.

Nutrition:
Calories: 301 Carbohydrates: 21g Fat: 17g Proteins: 8g

78. Wholesome Farm Salad

Preparation time: 15 minutes   Cooking time: 4 hours   Servings: 5

Ingredients:
- ½ cup hulled barley
- 2 beetroots
- 2 tbsp. sunflower seeds
- 6 cups romaine lettuce
- ½ cup scallions
- ½ cup coriander
- 2 tbsp. raisins
- ½ cup orange juice
- 1 tbsp. lemon juice
- Black pepper
- Himalayan pink salt

Directions:
1. In a large bowl, cover barley with water, then leave to soak for at least 3 hours.
2. Drain the barley water and add barley to a pot over high heat. Attach 2 cups of water and boil for 5 to 7 minutes, then turn heat to low and cover the pot. Simmer for 25 minutes or until the barley is tender but not soft. Drain and set aside to cool to room temperature.
3. Scrub the outside of the beets then cut each into quarters.
4. Put the beets in a medium pan and add water until it covers the beets. Set to a boil, then simmer partially covered. Stew for 30 minutes or until the beets are tender. Drain. Peel off the beets while they are still warm and cut them into bite-size pieces. Set aside.
5. Toast the sunflower seeds over medium high heat, stirring every so often, for 5 minutes or until barely toasted. Let cool on a plate.
6. Chop romaine, green onion, and cilantro.
7. In a large bowl, attach the barley and beets. Add romaine, green onions, cilantro, raisins, orange juice, lemon juice, a sprinkle of pepper, and a pinch of salt. Toss gently then sprinkle the toasted sunflower seeds over the salad.

Nutrition:
Calories: 245 Fat: 18.9g Carbohydrate: 15.9g Proteins: 6.4g

79. Spicy Chickpea Crunch

Preparation time: 5 minutes   Cooking time: 0 minutes   Servings: 2

Ingredients:
- 1 garlic clove
- 1 tbsp. sesame oil
- 2 tbsp. rice vinegar
- ½ tsp. hot sauce
- 2 tbsp. tamari
- 1 tsp. maple syrup
- 2 tsp. sesame seeds
- 2 cups spinach
- 1 can chickpeas
- 2 stalks celery
- 2 carrots
- ½ cucumber
- 2 green onions
- 1 ripe avocado
- 4 tbsp. walnuts

Directions:
1. Mince garlic and whisk with the oil, vinegar, hot sauce, tamari, maple syrup, and sesame seeds until combined. Refrigerate until ready to serve.

2. Evenly divide the spinach between two serving bowls.
3. Drain and rinse the chickpeas, then half it between the bowls.
4. Thinly slice the celery, carrots, cucumber, green onions, and chop the avocado. Divide evenly between each bowl.
5. Thinly slice or chop walnuts and sprinkle half over each bowl. Use a measuring spoon to pour 1 tbsp. of the previously prepared dressing into each bowl and serve promptly.

Nutrition:
Calories: 384 Fat: 14g Carbohydrates: 58g Fiber: 6g Proteins: 11g

80. Easy Italian Bowl

Preparation time: 15 minutes   Cooking time: 5 minutes   Servings: 5

Ingredients:
- 1 red onion
- 1 cup basil
- 12 ounces wheat spiral pasta
- 1 bag assorted frozen vegetables
- 1 cup balsamic vinaigrette
- Salt
- Pepper

Directions:
1. Finely dice onion and basil.
2. Boil water and cook the pasta. During the last 5 minutes of cooking, attach frozen vegetables to the pot. Drain the pasta and vegetables. Rinse under cold water until cool.
3. Move mixture to a large bowl. Add the onion, vinaigrette, and basil. Gently mix to coat. Add a pinch of salt and pepper. Can be served cold or room-temperature.

Nutrition:
Calories: 150 Fat: 7.3g Fiber: 6.1g Carbohydrates: 18g Proteins: 3.7g

81. Light Lemon Salad

Preparation time: 15 minutes   **Cooking time:** 20 minutes   Servings: 4

Ingredients:
- 1 bunch kale
- 1 bunch parsley
- 4 garlic cloves
- 2 tsp. avocado oil
- ¼ cup pitted Kalamata olives
- Grated zest and juice of 1 lemon
- Salt
- Pepper

Directions:
1. Esteem the kale, and chop finely. Roughly chop parsley and garlic.
2. Set a pot with water and heat to medium heat. Place a steamer tray over the pot and fill it with kale, parsley, and garlic. Cover and leave for 15 minutes.
3. Attach the oil to a pan over medium heat. Once the oil is hot, add the steamed greens. Cook and stir for 5 minutes.
4. Chop olives, then transfer with the greens to a bowl and add lemon zest and juice. Serve on toast with hummus and season with salt and pepper for the best experience!

Nutrition:
Calories: 141 Fat: 2g Carbohydrates: 22.5g Fiber: 2g Proteins: 4g

82. Cooked Cauliflower Bowl

Preparation time: 15 minutes   **Cooking time:** 20 minutes   Servings: 4

Ingredients:
- 1 head cauliflower
- ½ cup avocado oil
- 1¼ tsp. salt
- 1 tsp. pepper
- 1 green onion
- ⅓ cup raisins
- 1 tsp. lemon zest
- 1 tbsp. lemon juice
- 1 tsp. coriander powder
- 1 cup parsley
- ½ cup mint
- ¼ cup almond

Directions:

1. Set oven rack to lowest position and preheat to 475°F. Degrees.
2. Cut the cauliflower into small florets. Chop and save the core of the cauliflower.
3. Add cauliflower florets, 1 tablespoon oil, 1 teaspoon salt, and ½ teaspoon pepper to a bowl. Toss to coat.
4. Transfer to a baking pan and roast for 15 minutes or until florets are soft and browned on bottoms. Set aside and let cool.
5. While the florets are roasting, finely chop green onion and combine with raisins, lemon zest and juice, coriander, remaining ¼ cup oil, remaining ¼ teaspoon salt, and remaining ½ teaspoon pepper in a large bowl. Mix thoroughly and set aside.
6. Add cauliflower core to the blender and until finely chopped. Add to the bowl with dressing.
7. Add parsley and mint to the blender and pulse until coarsely chopped. Add to the bowl with dressing.
8. Finely slice almonds.
9. Add cooked cauliflower and almonds to bowl with dressing mixture and gently mix. Season with salt and pepper to taste. Serve.

Nutrition:
Calories: 231 Proteins: 14.9g Carbohydrates: 3.2g Fat: 18g Fiber: 1.1g

83. Seasoned Tofu Potato Salad

Preparation time: 15 minutes   **Cooking time:** 10 minutes   Servings: 8

Ingredients:
- 8 potatoes
- 1 package firm tofu
- 2 tbsp. yellow mustard
- 1 tbsp. Dijon mustard
- 4 cloves garlic
- 1 tbsp. fresh lime juice
- ½ tsp. salt
- ¼ cup pickle relish
- 4 large stalks celery
- 1 onion
- Pepper

Directions:
1. Roughly chop potatoes into chunks, then put in a large pot and add cold water to cover.
2. Set to a boil then lower heat to simmer the potatoes until just tender, 8 to 10 minutes. Drain potatoes and let cool.
3. Put the tofu, yellow mustard, Dijon mustard, chopped garlic, lime juice, and salt into a food processor and pulse until smooth and creamy.
4. Add the relish to the tofu mix and mix well.
5. Dice the celery, onion and add to the tofu bowl.
6. Chop potatoes into bite-sized pieces. Season with salt and pepper to taste. Gently mix until coated.
7. Secure bowl and refrigerate for at least 1 hour.

Nutrition:
Calories: 222 Fat: 6g Carbohydrates: 43g Fiber: 5g Proteins: 3g

84. Classic Potato Comfort

Preparation time: 10 minutes   **Cooking time:** 20 minutes   Servings: 4

Ingredients:
- 1 ½ cups long-grain rice
- ¼ cup roasted cashews
- 4 large potatoes
- 4 cups white mushrooms
- 1 clove garlic
- 4 cups vegetable broth
- ½ tsp. dried sage
- ½ tsp. dried marjoram
- ½ tsp. dried thyme
- 2 tbsp. fresh lemon juice
- ½ tsp. pepper
- Salt

Directions:
1. Cook the rice.
2. Set the cashews in a small bowl and cover with 1 cup water. Set aside to soak for 30 minutes.

3. Scrub the outside of the potatoes then chop into inch pieces. Slice the mushrooms, and finely chop garlic.
4. Set the potatoes in a pot and secure with water. Place to a boil, then lower the heat and simmer until the potatoes are very tender when skewered, about 20 minutes. Drain and set aside to cool.
5. In a pot, combine the rice, mushrooms, and vegetable broth. Set to a boil then reduce the heat and simmer until the mushrooms are soft, about 10 minutes. Set aside to cool.
6. Using a blender or handheld mixer, blend the mixture until smooth.
7. Put the blended mix back into the pot and add the sage, marjoram, thyme, garlic, lime juice, ⅛ teaspoon of the pepper, and a pinch of salt. Heat over medium heat for 10 minutes and stir occasionally.
8. Spill the cashews and their water into a clean blender. Add a pinch of salt and ¼ teaspoon pepper. Blend until there are no chunks. Dump the pecan butter in a bowl with the potatoes and mash together until smooth.
9. Serve on a plate with the potatoes and gravy spooned over top.

Nutrition:
Calories: 152 Fat: 10g Carbohydrates: 11.5g Fiber: 3g Proteins: 2g

85. Fried Zucchini

Preparation time: 10 minutes **Cooking time:** 20 minutes Servings: 4

Ingredients:
- 4 zucchinis
- ½ cup unsweetened almond milk
- 1 tsp. arrowroot powder
- 1 tsp. lemon juice
- ½ tsp. salt
- ½ cup panko
- ¼ cup hemp seeds
- ¼ cup nutritional yeast
- ½ tsp. garlic powder
- ¼ tsp. pepper
- ¼ tsp. red pepper flakes

Directions:
1. Slice the zucchini into rounds.
2. Warmth the oven to 375F and grease two large baking pans.
3. Put the zucchini in a bowl with the milk, arrowroot powder, lemon juice, and ¼ teaspoon salt. Toss to coat.
4. Mix the panko, hemp seeds, nutritional yeast, garlic powder, pepper, and crushed red pepper in a bowl. Add the zucchini in handfuls and toss to thoroughly coat.
5. Set the zucchini in an even layer on the baking pans. Bake for 20 minutes or until the zucchini is toasted.
6. Serve.

Nutrition:
Calories: 91 Fat: 1g Proteins: 4g Carbohydrates: 17g Fiber: 5g

86. Thick Sweet Potato Fries

Preparation time: 10 minutes **Cooking time:** 30 minutes Servings: 2

Ingredients:
- 2 sweet potatoes
- 1 tsp. garlic powder
- ½ tsp. cumin powder
- ½ tsp. chili powder
- ½ tsp. salt
- ½ tsp. black pepper

Directions:
1. Preheat the oven to 425F.
2. Peel and quarter sweet potatoes.
3. Set a pot halfway with water and place over medium heat. Put a steamer tray on top and fill with the potato. Cover and steam for 8 minutes.
4. Spread the potato evenly on a greased baking pan.
5. In a small bowl, whisk the garlic, cumin, chili powder, salt, and pepper. Whisk the spice mixture evenly over the sweet potatoes and toss to coat.

6. Cook for 10 minutes, then flip potatoes and cook for another 10 minutes. Potatoes should be soft and browned.

Nutrition:

Calories: 245 Fat: 18.9g Carbohydrate: 15.9g Proteins: 6.4g

87. Hot Wings with Ranch

Preparation time: 10 minutes **Cooking time:** 2 hours 30 minute Servings: 4

Ingredients:
- ½ cup chickpea flour
- ½ cup water
- 1 tsp. garlic powder
- ½ tsp. salt
- 1 head cauliflower, chopped
- 1 tsp. avocado oil
- ⅔ cup hot sauce
- ½ cup roasted cashews
- 4 tsp. lime juice
- ½ tsp. dill
- ¼ tsp. garlic powder
- ¼ tsp. paprika
- Salt
- Pepper

Directions:
1. Set the cashews in a bowl and add 2 tsp. of lime juice. Add enough water to cover cashews and a little more. Let soak for 2 hours, then drain and wash well.
2. In a strong blender, add cashews, ¼ cup water, dill, garlic powder, paprika, 2 tsp. lime juice, salt, and pepper to taste. Blend until smooth.
3. Preheat the oven to 450F. Grease a large baking tray.
4. Chop the cauliflower into bite-sized florets.
5. Whisk together the flour, water, garlic powder, and salt.
6. Dip the florets in the batter, coating each piece thoroughly. Place carefully on the baking tray and cook for 8 minutes. Flip florets over and cook for another 8 minutes.
7. While the cauliflower is cooking, whisk together the oil and hot sauce.
8. When the cauliflower is done, move the florets to the bowl with the sauce and coat thoroughly. Place the sauce-covered cauliflower back on the baking sheet and cook for 25 minutes or until crispy.
9. Serve the cauliflower with cold sauce.

Nutrition:

Calories: 141 Fat: 2g Carbohydrates: 22.5g Fiber: 2g Proteins: 4g

88. Breaded Tempeh Bites

Preparation time: 10 minutes **Cooking time:** 35 minutes Servings: 4

Ingredients:
- 8 oz. package tempeh
- ¼ cup oat milk
- ¼ cup nutritional yeast
- 1 tbsp. pre-blended spice mix
- 1 tsp. arrowroot powder
- 1 tsp. fresh lime juice
- ¼ tsp. pepper
- ¼ tsp. hot sauce
- ¼ tsp. salt
- 1 cup panko

Directions:
1. Preheat the oven to 400F. Grease a large baking pan.
2. Cut the tempeh in half and cut into 8 pieces. Squish each piece lightly to flatten slightly.
3. In a bowl, combine the milk, nutritional yeast, seasoning blend, arrowroot powder, lime juice, pepper, hot sauce, and salt. Add the tempeh bits and let soak for 5 minutes. Make sure each piece is evenly coated.
4. Pour the panko on a plate. Dip each piece of tempeh from the batter to roll in the panko. Place on the prepared baking pan.
5. Cook for 15 minutes. Flip all pieces, and then cook for another 15 minutes or until golden brown.

Nutrition:

Calories: 288 Fat: 11.11g Carbohydrates: 45.3g Proteins: 4.4g

89. Cumin Chili Chickpeas

Preparation time: 10 minutes **Cooking time:** 45 minutes Servings: 6

Ingredients:
- 1 can chickpeas
- 1 tbsp. paprika powder
- 1 tbsp. cumin powder
- 2 tsp. red chili flakes
- 2 tbsp. maple syrup
- 3 tbsp. lemon juice
- 1 tbsp. avocado oil
- Sea salt
- Black pepper

Directions:
1. Preheat the oven to 395F.
2. Drain and wash the chickpeas, then spread them on a large oven pan.
3. Mix the paprika, cumin, chili flakes, and a pinch of salt and pepper. Even powder over the chickpeas.
4. Merge together the maple syrup, lemon juice, and oil, then pour over the chickpeas. Set the mixture to make sure the chickpeas are fully coated.
5. Cook for 45 minutes, or until browned and crisp.

Nutrition:
Calories: 268 Carbohydrates: 33g Fat: 8g Proteins: 10g

90. Summer Sushi

Preparation time: 10 minutes **Cooking time:** 10 minutes Servings: 6

Ingredients:
- 2 cucumbers
- 2 avocados
- 4 tbsp. lime juice
- 2 tbsp. extra-virgin olive oil
- Sea salt
- Black pepper

Directions:
1. Peel the cucumber skin off and throw it away.
2. Peel or slice each cucumber lengthwise, going from the bottom to the top. Discard the very middle of the cucumber, as it is not strong enough to shape.
3. After the cucumbers are sliced, take each slice and tightly roll it from the bottom up.
4. Slice opens the avocado and discards the pit. Cut the avocado flesh into tiny squares and put inside the cucumber circles. Cram as much in as possible for a more stable roll.
5. After you've completed your rolls, lightly cover with lime juice and olive oil. Drizzle a pinch of salt and pepper on top and serve!

Nutrition:
Calories: 523 Carbohydrates: 57.6g Proteins: 7.5g Fat: 37.6g

91. Special Cheese Board

Preparation time: 10 minutes **Cooking time:** 30 minutes Servings: 8

Ingredients:
- 2 cups almond flour
- 4 tbsp. onion powder
- Water
- 1 tsp. light soy sauce
- 1 tbsp. poppy seeds
- 5 tsp. agar agar powder
- ½ cup bell pepper
- ½ cup raw cashews
- 1⅓ cup nutritional yeast
- 4 tbsp. lemon juice
- ½ tsp. mustard

Directions:
1. Preheat the oven to 350F.
2. To make the crackers, mix the flour, 3 tbsp. onion powder, 3 tbsp. water, soy sauce, and poppy seeds. Form into a ball.
3. Secure a baking tray with parchment paper and place the ball on top. Press it down as flat as possible, and then place another piece of parchment sheet on top.

4. On top of the second sheet of parchment, use a rolling pin to roll the cracker mix to about ¼th inch thick.
5. Remove the second sheet of parchment and cook in the oven for about 15 minutes.
6. When the crackers are done baking, let cool and cut into cracker-sized pieces. Store in an airtight container.
7. Put the agar agar and 1 ½ cups of water into a small pot over high heat. Wait for it to boil and whisk continuously until the mixture becomes thick like custard.
8. Remove from heat and scoop into a blender.
9. Roughly chop pepper and add to the blender along with the cashews, nutritional yeast, lemon juice, 2 tsp. onion powder, and mustard. Pulse until smooth.
10. Pour the blended mix into a bread pan lined with parchment paper and refrigerate for at least 30 minutes before serving.

Nutrition:
Calories: 46 Fat: 1g Proteins: 3g Carbohydrates: 7g Fiber: 1g

92. Three-Ingredient Flatbread

Preparation time: 10 minutes **Cooking time:** 25 minutes Servings: 5

Ingredients:
- 1 cup tri-color quinoa
- 1½ cups water
- 1 tsp. onion powder

Directions:
1. Before starting, preheat the oven to 400F.
2. In a blender, all ingredients. Blend until smooth with no lumps.
3. Set a baking pan with parchment paper (make sure the pan has a small lip).
4. Evenly spread the quinoa blend on the baking sheet and put in the oven for 20-25 minutes.
5. Remove from the oven and allow cooling.

Nutrition:
Calories: 188.4 Fat: 7.7g Carbohydrates: 29.3g Proteins: 3.7g Fiber: 8.2g

93. Spicy Homemade Tortilla Chips

Preparation time: 10 minutes **Cooking time:** 16 minutes Servings: 6

Ingredients:
- 12 corn tortillas
- 1 tsp. olive oil
- ¼ tsp. chili powder
- ¼ tsp. cumin powder
- ¼ tsp. garlic powder
- ¼ tsp. paprika powder
- Himalayan sea salt

Directions:
1. Before starting, preheat the oven to 425F.
2. Set 2 large baking pans with parchment paper.
3. Slice each tortilla into 6 triangles, then place on the baking pans, trying not to overlap. Set in the oven and cook for 10 minutes.
4. Take the baking pans out of the oven and delicately brush oil over the surface side of the chips (use only a little, otherwise the chips won't be crispy)
5. Mix the spices and salt together and sprinkle over the chips.
6. Put the chips back in the oven for another 6 minutes, or until crispy and golden.

Nutrition:
Calories: 142 Fat: 8g Carbohydrate: 14g Proteins: 4g

94. Healthy Cereal Bars

Preparation time: 10 minutes **Cooking time:** 30 minutes Servings: 9

Ingredients:
- ½ cup toasted almonds
- 1 ½ cup oats
- ½ cup almond flour
- ½ cup pure maple syrup
- ½ cup raisins
- ¼ cup almond butter

- 2 tablespoons chia seeds
- 1 tbsp. fractionated coconut oil
- 1 tsp. vanilla extract
- ½ tsp. cinnamon powder
- ¼ tsp. Himalayan pink sea salt
- ⅛ tsp. nutmeg powder

Directions:
1. Go ahead and preheat the oven to 325F.
2. Use an 8x8 inch baking tin and grease and line with non-stick parchment paper.
3. Slice the almonds and add to a large bowl alongside the oats, almond flour, syrup, raisins, almond butter, chia seeds, oil, vanilla, cinnamon, salt, and nutmeg. Mix until it all sticks together.
4. Pat the almond mix into the pan, making sure the top is even. Put in the oven for 25 to 30 minutes, or until the edges of the pan are golden.
5. Allow to cool.

Nutrition:
Calories: 68 Fat: 1g Proteins: 3g Carbohydrates: 15g Fiber: 4g

95. Black Bean Taquitos

Preparation time: 10 minutes **Cooking time:** 21 minutes Servings: 12

Ingredients:
- Olive oil
- 1 onion
- 1 poblano chili pepper
- 1 jalapeño Chili pepper
- 4 garlic cloves
- 1 can black beans
- ½ cup cilantro leaves
- 1 tsp. chili powder
- 1 tsp. cumin powder
- 1 tsp. sea salt
- 24 corn tortillas

Directions:
1. Preheat your oven to 400F.
2. Set the parchment paper then grease with oil.
3. Chop your onion into quarters. Half both peppers and deseed them before chopping into quarters.
4. Using a food processor, add onion, poblano pepper, jalapeño pepper, and garlic. Use the chopping blade and pulse 3 times before adding the black beans, cilantro, chili powder, cumin, and salt.
5. Pulse another 3 times or until the mixture is finely chopped (you can pulse more if you want a smoother mix).
6. Put the tortillas on a pan and heat them in the oven for about a minute, or until soft and pliable.
7. Smear a large tablespoon of bean mix across each tortilla. Tightly roll like a burrito with open edges and put on a baking pan with the edge facing down. Leave a smidge of space between each tortilla and cook for 20 minutes or until golden.

Nutrition:
Calories: 152 Fat: 10g Carbohydrates: 11.5g Fiber: 3g Proteins: 2g

96. Vegetable Tacos

Preparation time: 10 minutes **Cooking time:** 23 minutes Servings: 4

Ingredients:
- 1 head of cauliflower
- 1 sweet potato
- 1 onion
- 2 tbsp. olive oil
- ⅛ tsp. Himalayan salt
- ⅛ tsp. black pepper
- 1 can chickpeas
- ½ cup BBQ

Directions:
1. Preheat your oven to 425F and put a sheet of parchment paper on a large baking tray.
2. Chop the cauliflower into small florets, the sweet potato into inch sized cubes, and dice the onion into small pieces.
3. Evenly place the cauliflower, sweet potato, and onion across the baking tray. Sprinkle oil, salt, and pepper across and mix to coat. Set in the oven for 15 minutes.

4. Set the tray out of the oven and dump the chickpeas on top. Pour ½ cup of BBQ sauce on top and stir to coat. Bake for another 8 minutes until the vegetables are soft.

Nutrition:

Calories: 112 Fat: 6g Carbohydrates: 9g Fiber: 1.5g Proteins: 7g

97. Tomato Basil Soup

Preparation time: 10 minutes **Cooking time:** 63 minutes Servings: 6

Ingredients:
- 3 pounds of halved tomatoes
- 1 cup of canned crushed tomatoes
- 2-3 chopped carrots
- 2 chopped yellow onions
- 5 minced garlic cloves
- 2 ounces of basil leaves
- 2 teaspoons of thyme leaves
- 1 teaspoon of dried oregano
- ½ teaspoon of ground cumin
- ½ teaspoon of paprika
- 2 ½ cups of water
- Fresh lime juice, to taste
- Salt, to taste
- Black Pepper, to taste

Directions:
1. Preheat your oven to 450F.
2. Mix carrots with tomatoes in a large bowl. Add salt, black pepper, and toss.
3. Put the vegetable mixture on the baking sheet in a single layer. Roast for 30 minutes, then set aside for 10 minutes.
4. Transfer the roasted vegetables in a food processor or a blender, add just a little water, and blend.
5. Place a large stockpot on medium heat. Add the chopped onions, water and simmer for 3 minutes, then add minced garlic and cook until golden.
6. Pour the blended mixture into the stockpot. Add in 2 ½ cups of water, the canned tomatoes, thyme, basil, and other seasonings. Set it to a boil, reduce to low heat, and cover. Simmer for about 20 minutes.
7. Serve with a splash of lime juice* and enjoy your Tomato Basil Soup!

Nutrition:

Calories: 104.9 Carbohydrates: 23.4g Proteins: 4.3g Fat: 0.8g

98. Pearl Couscous Salad

Preparation time: 10 minutes **Cooking time:** 30 minutes Servings: 5

Ingredients:
- ¾ cup of whole-wheat pearl couscous
- 1 ½ cups of quartered grape tomatoes
- ¾ pound of thin asparagus spears
- ¼ cup of chopped red onion
- 1 ½ juiced lemons
- 2 tablespoons of chopped parsley
- Sea salt, to taste
- Black pepper, to taste

Directions:
1. Pour water into a large pot, add salt, and bring it to a boil. Attach in asparagus and cook for 3 minutes until tender.
2. Set out asparagus with a slotted spoon and clean it under cold running water.
3. Cook couscous in the boiling water according to package directions.
4. Set the cooked asparagus into ½-inch pieces.
5. Drain couscous and wash it under cold running water. Set it in a large bowl.
6. Attach vegetables, lemon juice, parsley, pepper, and salt to the bowl. Toss it.
7. Serve and enjoy your Pearl Couscous Salad!

Nutrition:

Calories: 170 Carbohydrates: 30g Proteins: 6.5g Fat: 4g

99. Vegan Tomato Soup

Preparation time: 10 minutes **Cooking time:** 1 hour 30 minutes Servings: 4

Ingredients:

- 4 lbs. tomatoes
- 3 shallots, peeled
- 5 garlic cloves, peeled
- 2 teaspoons fresh thyme leaves
- 2 tablespoons olive oil
- Salt and black pepper, to taste
- ½ cup raw cashews
- 1 tablespoon tomato paste
- ½ cup basil leaves, packed
- 3 cups vegetable stock
- 1 tablespoon balsamic vinegar

Directions:
1. Preheat your oven to 350F. Layer a baking sheet with parchment paper.
2. Spread the tomato pieces in the baking and add garlic cloves on top.
3. Add shallots around the tomato pieces.
4. Set olive oil, black pepper and salt over the veggies.
5. Roast these veggies for 1 hour, then allow them to cool.
6. Blend the roasted tomatoes with cashews, tomato paste, basil, and vegetable stock in a blender until smooth.
7. Transfer this soup to a cooking pan and cook to a boil.
8. Stir in vinegar and garnish with basil and olive oil.
9. Serve warm.

Nutrition:
Calories: 384 Fat: 14g Carbohydrates: 58g Fiber: 6g

100. Butternut Squash Chickpea Stew

Preparation time: 10 minutes **Cooking time:** 26 minutes Servings: 6

Ingredients:
- 1 tablespoon olive oil
- 1 medium white onion, chopped
- 6 garlic cloves, minced
- 2 teaspoons cumin
- 1 teaspoon cinnamon
- 1 teaspoon ground turmeric
- ¼ teaspoon cayenne pepper
- 1 (28-ounce) can crushed tomatoes
- 2½ cups vegetable broth
- 1 (15-ounce) can chickpeas, rinsed
- 4 cups butternut squash, cubed
- 1 cup green lentils, rinsed
- ½ teaspoon salt
- Black pepper, to taste
- fresh juice of ½ lemon
- ⅓ cup cilantro, chopped
- Basil leaves, chopped

Directions:
1. Sauté garlic and onion with oil in a suitable pot over medium high heat for 5 minutes.
2. Stir in cayenne, turmeric, cinnamon and cumin then sauté for 30 seconds.
3. Add black pepper, salt, and lentils. Butternut squash, chickpeas, broth and tomatoes.
4. Cook to a boil, reduce its heat then cover and cook for 20 minutes.
5. Add basil, cilantro and lemon juice.
6. Serve warm.

Nutrition:
Calories: 142 Fat: 8g Carbohydrate: 14g Proteins: 4g

Dinner

101. Sweet and Sour Tempeh

Preparation time: 10 minutes Cooking time: 8 minutes Servings: 4

Ingredients:
- 1 cup pineapple juice
- 1 tablespoon unseasoned rice vinegar
- 1 tablespoon soy sauce
- 1 tablespoon cornstarch
- 2 tablespoons coconut oil
- 1-pound tempeh, cut into thin strips
- 6 green onions
- 1 green bell pepper, diced
- 4 garlic cloves, minced
- 2 cups prepared brown or white rice

Directions:
1. Blend pineapple juice, rice vinegar, soy sauce, and cornstarch and set aside.
2. In a wok or large sauté pan, warmth the coconut oil over medium-high heat until it shimmers. Add the tempeh, green onions, and bell pepper, and cook until vegetables soften about 5 minutes.
3. Cook garlic. Set in sauce and cook until it thickens. Serve over rice.

Nutrition:
Calories: 244 Fat: 2g Proteins: 11g Carbohydrates: 50g Fiber: 10g

102. Fried Seitan Fingers

Preparation time: 15 minutes Cooking time: 10 minutes Servings: 4

Ingredients:
- 1 cup all-purpose flour
- 1 teaspoon garlic powder
- 1 teaspoon onion powder
- Pinch of cayenne pepper
- 1 teaspoon dried thyme
- ½ teaspoon sea salt
- ½ teaspoon freshly ground black pepper
- 1 cup soy milk
- 1 tablespoon lemon juice
- 2 tablespoons baking powder
- 2 tablespoons olive oil
- 8 ounces Seitan

Directions:
1. In a shallow dish, incorporate the flour, garlic powder, onion powder, cayenne, thyme, salt, and black pepper, whisking to mix thoroughly. In another shallow dish, whisk together the soy milk, lemon juice, and baking powder.
2. In a sauté pan, cook the olive oil over medium-high heat. Set each piece of seitan in the flour mixture, tapping off any excess flour. Next, dip the seitan in the soymilk mixture and then back into the flour mixture.
3. Fry for 4 minutes per side. Blot on paper towels before serving.

Nutrition:
Calories: 388 Fat: 19g Carbohydrates: 45g Fiber: 12g Sugar: 13g

103. Crusty Grilled Corn

Preparation time: 10 minutes   Cooking time: 15 minutes   Servings: 4

Ingredients:
- 2 corn cobs
- ⅓ cup Vegenaise
- 1 small handful cilantro
- ½ cup breadcrumbs
- 1 teaspoon lemon juice

Directions:
1. Preheat the gas grill on high heat.
2. Add corn grill to the grill and continue grilling until it turns golden-brown on all sides.
3. Mix the Vegenaise, cilantro, breadcrumbs, and lemon juice in a bowl.
4. Add grilled corn cobs to the crumbs mixture.
5. Toss well then serve.

Nutrition:
Calories: 253 Fat: 13g Proteins: 31g Fiber: 0g Carbohydrates: 3g

104. Grilled Carrots with Chickpea Salad

Preparation time: 10 minutes.   **Cooking time:** 5 minutes.   Servings: 8

Ingredients:
- 8 large carrots
- 1 tablespoon oil
- 1(½) teaspoon salt
- 1 teaspoon dried oregano
- 1 teaspoon dried thyme
- 2 teaspoons paprika powder
- 1(½) tablespoon soy sauce
- ½ cup of water
- Chickpea salad:
- 14 ounces canned chickpeas
- 3 medium pickles
- 1 small onion
- A big handful of lettuce
- 1 teaspoon apple cider vinegar
- ½ teaspoon dried oregano
- ½ teaspoon salt
- Ground black pepper to taste
- ½ cup vegan cream

Directions:
1. Toss the carrots with all the ingredients in a bowl.
2. Thread one carrot on a stick and place it on a plate.
3. Preheat the grill over high heat.
4. Grill the carrots for 2 minutes per side on the grill.
5. Toss the ingredients for the salad in a large salad bowl.
6. Slice grilled carrots and add them on top of the salad.
7. Serve fresh.

Nutrition:
Calories: 661 Fat: 68g Carbohydrates: 7g Fiber: 2g Proteins: 4g

105. Grilled Avocado Guacamole

Preparation time: 10 minutes   Cooking time: 22 minutes   Servings: 4

Ingredients:
- ½ teaspoon olive oil
- 1 lime, halved

- ½ onion, halved
- 1 serrano chili, halved, stemmed, and seeded
- 3 Haas avocados, skin on
- 2-3 tablespoons fresh cilantro, chopped
- ½ teaspoon smoked salt

Directions:
1. Preheat the grill over medium heat.
2. Brush the grilling grates with olive oil and place chili, onion, and lime on them.
3. Grill the onion for 10 minutes, chili for 5 minutes, and lime for 2 minutes.
4. Transfer the veggies to a large bowl.
5. Now cut the avocados in half and grill them for 5 minutes.
6. Mash the flesh of the grilled avocado in a bowl.
7. Chop the other grilled veggies and add them to the avocado mash.
8. Stir in the remaining ingredients and merge well. Serve.

Nutrition:
Calories: 165 Fat: 17g Carbohydrates: 4g Fiber: 1g Proteins: 1g

106. Spinach and Dill Pasta Salad

Preparation time: 5 minutes Cooking time: 0 minutes Servings: 4

Ingredients:

For the salad:
- 3 cups cooked whole-wheat fusilli
- 2 cups cherry tomatoes, halved
- ½ cup vegan cheese, shredded
- 4 cups spinach, chopped
- 2 cups edamame, thawed
- 1 large red onion, finely chopped

For the dressing:
- 2 tablespoons white wine vinegar
- ½ teaspoon dried dill
- 2 tablespoons extra-virgin olive oil
- Salt to taste
- Pepper to taste

Directions:
1. To make the dressing: Attach all the ingredients for dressing into a bowl and whisk well. Set aside for a while for the flavors to set in.
2. To make the salad: Add all the ingredients of the salad to a bowl. Toss well. Drizzle dressing on top. Toss well. Divide into 4 plates and serve.

Nutrition:
Calories: 684 Fat: 33.6g Carbohydrate: 69.5g

107. Italian Veggie Salad

Preparation time: 10 minutes Cooking time: 0 minutes Servings: 8

Ingredients:

For the salad:
- 1 cup fresh baby carrots, quartered lengthwise
- 1 celery rib, sliced
- 3 large mushrooms, thinly sliced
- 1 cup cauliflower florets, bite-sized, blanched
- 1 cup broccoli florets, blanched
- 1 cup thinly sliced radish
- 4–5 ounces hearts of romaine salad mix to serve
- For the dressing:
- ½ package Italian salad dressing mix
- 3 tablespoons white vinegar
- 3 tablespoons water
- 3 tablespoons olive oil
- 3-4 pepperoncini, chopped

Directions:
1. To make the salad: Add all the ingredients of the salad except hearts of romaine to a bowl and toss.
2. To make the dressing: Attach all the ingredients of the dressing in a small bowl. Whisk well. Pour dressing over salad and toss well. Refrigerate for a couple of hours. Place romaine in a large bowl. Place the chilled salad over it and serve.

Nutrition:
Calories: 84 Fat: 6.7g Carbohydrate: 5g

108. Spinach and Mashed Tofu Salad

Preparation time: 20 minutes　　Cooking time: 0 minutes　　Servings: 4

Ingredients:
- 2(8-ounces) blocks firm tofu, drained
- 4 cups baby spinach leaves
- 4 tablespoons cashew butter
- 1(½) tablespoon soy sauce
- 1 tablespoon ginger, chopped
- 1 teaspoon red miso paste
- 2 tablespoons sesame seeds
- 1 teaspoon organic orange zest
- 1 teaspoon nori flakes
- 2 tablespoons water

Directions:
1. In a bowl, merge the mashed tofu with the spinach leaves.
2. Merge the remaining ingredients in another small bowl and, if desired, add the optional water for a smoother dressing.
3. Spill this dressing over the mashed tofu and spinach leaves.
4. Set the bowl to the fridge and allow the salad to chill. Enjoy!

Nutrition:
Calories: 623 Fat: 30.5g Carbohydrate: 48g

109. Super Summer Salad

Preparation time: 10 minutes.　　Cooking time: 0 minutes.　　Servings: 2

Ingredients:
Dressing:
- 1 tablespoon olive oil
- ¼ cup chopped basil
- 1 teaspoon lemon juice
- ¼ teaspoon salt
- 1 medium avocado, halved, diced
- ¼ cup water

Salad:
- ¼ cup dry chickpeas
- ¼ cup dry red kidney beans
- 4 cups raw kale, shredded
- 2 cups Brussels sprouts, shredded
- 2 radishes, thinly sliced
- 1 tablespoon walnuts, chopped
- 1 teaspoon flax seeds
- Salt and pepper to taste

Directions:
1. Prepare the chickpeas and kidney beans according to the method.
2. Soak the flaxseeds according to the method and then drain excess water.
3. Attach the olive oil, basil, lemon juice, salt, and half of the avocado to a food processor or blender, and pulse at low speed. Set the dressing to a small bowl and set it aside.
4. Combine the kale, Brussels sprouts, cooked chickpeas, kidney beans, radishes, walnuts, and the remaining avocado in a large bowl and mix thoroughly.
5. Store the mixture, or serve with the dressing and flaxseeds, and enjoy!

Nutrition:
Calories: 266 Fat: 26.6g Carbohydrates: 8.8g Fiber: 6.8g Proteins: 2g

110. Roasted Almond Protein Salad

Preparation time: 30 minutes　　Cooking time: 0 minutes　　Servings: 4

Ingredients:
- ½ cup dry quinoa
- ½ cup dry navy beans
- ½ cup dry chickpeas
- ½ cup raw whole almonds
- 1 teaspoon extra-virgin olive oil
- ½ teaspoon salt
- ½ teaspoon paprika
- ½ teaspoon cayenne
- Dash of chili powder
- 4 cups spinach, fresh or frozen
- ¼ cup purple onion, chopped

Directions:
1. Prepare the quinoa according to the recipe. Store in the fridge for now. Prepare the beans according to the method. Store in the fridge for now. Set the almonds, olive oil, salt, and spices in a large bowl, and stir until the ingredients are evenly coated.
2. Set a skillet over medium-high heat and transfer the almond mixture to the heated skillet.
3. Roast while stirring. Stir frequently to prevent burning.
4. Set off the heat and toss the cooked and chilled quinoa and beans, onions, spinach, or mixed greens in the skillet. Stir well and set the roasted almond salad to a bowl.
5. Enjoy!

Nutrition:
Calories: 347 Fat: 10.5g Carbohydrate: 49.2g Fiber: 14.7g

111. Lentil, Lemon and Mushroom Salad

Preparation time: 10 minutes   **Cooking time:** 10-15 minutes   Servings: 2

Ingredients:
- ½ cup dry lentils of choice
- 2 cups vegetable broth
- 3 cups mushrooms, thickly sliced
- 1 cup sweet or purple onion, chopped
- 4 teaspoons extra-virgin olive oil
- 2 tablespoons garlic powder
- ¼ teaspoon chili flakes
- 1 tablespoon lemon juice
- 2 tablespoons cilantro, chopped
- ½ cup arugula
- ¼ teaspoon salt
- ¼ teaspoon pepper

Directions:
1. Sprout the lentils according to the method. (Don't cook them).
2. Place the vegetable stock in a deep saucepan and bring it to a boil.
3. Add the lentils to the boiling broth, cover the pan, and cook for about 5 minutes over low heat until the lentils are a bit tender.
4. Remove the pan from heat and drain the excess water.
5. Set a frying pan over high heat and attach 2 tablespoons of olive oil.
6. Add the onions, garlic, and chili flakes, and cook until the onions are almost translucent, around 5 to 10 minutes while stirring.
7. Attach the mushrooms to the frying pan and mix in thoroughly. Continue cooking until the onions are completely translucent and the mushrooms have softened; remove the pan from the heat.
8. Mix the lentils, onions, mushrooms, and garlic in a large bowl.
9. Attach the lemon juice and the remaining olive oil. Toss or stir to combine everything thoroughly.
10. Serve the mushroom/onion mixture over some arugula in a bowl, adding salt and pepper to taste, or store and enjoy later!

Nutrition:
Calories: 365 Fat: 11.7g Carbohydrates: 45.2g Proteins: 22.8g

112. Sweet Potato and Black Bean Protein Salad

Preparation time: 15 minutes.   **Cooking time:** 400 minutes.   Servings: 2

Ingredients:
- 1 cup dry black beans
- 4 cups of spinach
- 1 medium sweet potato
- 1 cup purple onion, chopped
- 2 tablespoons olive oil
- 2 tablespoons lime juice
- 1 tablespoon minced garlic
- ½ tablespoon chili powder
- ¼ teaspoon cayenne
- ¼ cup parsley
- ¼ teaspoons salt
- ¼ teaspoons pepper

Directions:
1. Prepare the black beans according to the method.
2. Preheat the oven to 400F.

3. Cut the sweet potato into ¼-inch cubes and put these in a medium-sized bowl. Add the onions, 1 tablespoon of olive oil, and salt to taste.
4. Toss the ingredients until the sweet potatoes and onions are completely coated.
5. Transfer the ingredients to a baking sheet lined with parchment paper and spread them out in a single layer.
6. Bring the baking sheet in the oven and roast until the sweet potatoes start to turn brown and crispy, around 40 minutes.
7. Meanwhile, combine the remaining olive oil, lime juice, garlic, chili powder, and cayenne thoroughly in a large bowl, until no lumps remain.
8. Detach the sweet potatoes and onions from the oven and transfer them to the large bowl.
9. Add the cooked black beans, parsley, and a pinch of salt.
10. Toss everything until well combined.
11. Then mix in the spinach and serve in desired portions with additional salt and pepper.
12. Store or enjoy!

Nutrition:
Calories: 558 Fat: 6.2g Carbohydrate: 84g Fiber: 20.4g

113. Lentil Radish Salad

Preparation time: 15 minutes   Cooking time: 0 minutes   Servings: 3

Ingredients:

Dressing:
- 1 tablespoon extra-virgin olive oil
- 1 tablespoon lemon juice
- 1 tablespoon maple syrup
- 1 tablespoon water
- ½ tablespoon sesame oil
- 1 tablespoon miso paste, yellow or white
- ¼ teaspoon salt
- ¼ teaspoons Pepper

Salad:
- ½ cup dry chickpeas
- ¼ cup dry green
- 1 (14-ounce) pack of silken tofu
- 5 cups mixed greens, fresh or frozen
- 2 radishes, thinly sliced
- ½ cup cherry tomatoes, halved
- ¼ cup roasted sesame seeds

Directions:
1. Prepare the chickpeas according to the method.
2. Prepare the lentils according to the method.
3. Set all the ingredients for the dressing in a blender or food processor. Mix on low until smooth, while adding water until it reaches the desired consistency.
4. Add salt, pepper (to taste), and optionally more water to the dressing; set aside.
5. Cut the tofu into bite-sized cubes.
6. Combine the mixed greens, tofu, lentils, chickpeas, radishes, and tomatoes in a large bowl.
7. Add the dressing and mix everything until it is coated evenly.
8. Top with the optional roasted sesame seeds, if desired.
9. Refrigerate before serving and enjoy, or store for later!

Nutrition:
Calories: 621 Fat: 19.6g Carbohydrates: 82.7g Fiber: 26.1g

114. Jicama and Spinach Salad Recipe

Preparation time: 10 minutes   Cooking time: 20 minutes   Servings: 4

Ingredients:

Salad:
- 10 ounces baby spinach, washed and dried
- 16 grape or cherry tomatoes
- 1 jicama
- Green or Kalamata olives, chopped
- 8 teaspoons walnuts, chopped
- 1 teaspoon raw or roasted sunflower seeds

Dressing:
- 1 heaping tablespoon Dijon mustard
- Dash cayenne pepper to taste
- 2 tablespoons maple syrup
- 2 garlic cloves, minced
- 1 to 2 tablespoons water
- ¼ teaspoons sea salt

Directions:
1. For the salad: Divide the baby spinach onto 4 salad plates. Set each serving with ¼ of the jicama, ¼ of the chopped olives, and 4 tomatoes. Sprinkle 1 teaspoon of the sunflower seeds and 2 teaspoons of the walnuts.
2. For the dressing: In a small mixing bowl, whisk all the ingredients together until emulsified. Check the taste and add more maple syrup for sweetness. Drizzle 1(½) tablespoon of the dressing over each salad and serve.

Nutrition:
Calories: 196 Fat: 2g Proteins: 7g Carbohydrates: 28g Fiber: 12g

115. High-Protein Salad

Preparation time: 5 minutes. Cooking time: 0 minutes. Servings: 4

Ingredients:
Salad:
- 1(15-ounces) can green kidney beans
- 4 tablespoons capers
- 4 handfuls arugula
- 4(15-ounces) can lentils

Dressing:
- 1 tablespoon caper brine
- 1 tablespoon tamari
- 1 tablespoon balsamic vinegar
- 2 tablespoons peanut butter
- 2 tablespoons hot sauce
- 1 tablespoon tahini

Directions:
1. For the dressing: In a bowl, spill together all the ingredients until they come together to form a smooth dressing.
2. For the salad: Mix the beans, arugula, capers, and lentils. Top with the dressing and serve.

Nutrition:
Calories: 205 Fat: 2g Proteins: 13g Carbohydrates: 31g Fiber: 17g

116. Mussels in Red Wine Sauce

Preparation time: 5 minutes Cooking time: 3 minutes Servings: 2

Ingredients:
- 800g mussels
- 2 x 400g tins of chopped tomatoes
- 25g butter
- 1 fresh chives, chopped
- 1 fresh parsley, chopped
- 1 bird's-eye chili, finely chopped
- 4 cloves of garlic, crushed
- 400mls red wine
- Juice of 1 lemon

Directions:
1. Wash the mussels, remove their beards, and set them aside. Warmth the butter in a large saucepan and add in the red wine. Reduce the heat and add the parsley, chives, chili, and garlic whilst stirring. Add in the tomatoes, lemon juice, and mussels. Cover the saucepan and cook for 2-3 minutes.
2. Remove the saucepan from the heat and take out any mussels which haven't opened and discard them. Serve and eat immediately.

Nutrition:
Calories: 364 Carbohydrates: 3.3g Fat: 4.9g Proteins: 8g

117. Roast Balsamic Vegetables

Preparation time: 10 minutes **Cooking time: 45 minutes** Servings: 4

Ingredients:
- 4 tomatoes, chopped 2 red onions, chopped
- 3 sweet potatoes, peeled and chopped

- 100g red chicory (or if unavailable, use yellow)
- 100g kale, finely chopped
- 300g potatoes, peeled and chopped
- 5 stalks of celery, chopped
- 1 bird's-eye chili, de-seeded and finely chopped
- 2g fresh parsley, chopped
- 2gs fresh coriander (cilantro) chopped
- 3 teaspoons olive oil
- 2 teaspoons balsamic vinegar
- 1 teaspoon mustard Sea salt
- Freshly ground black pepper

Directions:
1. Place the olive oil, balsamic, mustard, parsley, and coriander (cilantro) into a bowl and mix well.
2. Toss all the remaining ingredients into the dressing and season with salt and pepper.
3. Transfer the vegetables to an ovenproof dish and cook in the oven at 200C/400F for 45 minutes.

Nutrition:
Calories: 98 Fiber: 2g Proteins: 3g Carbohydrates: 3.1g

118. Vegan Caesar Salad

Preparation time: 20 minutes **Cooking time:** 1 hours 20 minutes Servings: 4

Ingredients:
- 1 15-oz can chickpeas
- ½ tsp. grated lemon zest
- 1 tbsp. olive oil
- Salt and pepper
- ¼ c. olive oil
- 1 tsp. grated lemon zest plus ⅓ cup lemon juice
- ¼ c. tahini
- 2 tsp. capers plus 1 tsp caper brine
- 1 small clove garlic, finely grated
- 1 tbsp. nutritional yeast
- 1 tbsp. Dijon mustard
- 3 tbsp. olive oil
- 4 thick slices bread
- 2 small red onions, cut into thick rounds
- 2 heads gem lettuce or romaine hearts, leaves separated
- 2 bunches small radishes
- 1 clove garlic, cut in half

Directions:
Crispy Chickpeas:
1. Preheat the oven to 425 degrees Fahrenheit. Rinse the chickpeas and pat them dry with paper towels, removing any loose skins.
2. Toss chickpeas with olive oil and ¼ teaspoon salt and pepper on a rimmed baking sheet. Roast for 30 to 40 minutes, tossing occasionally, until crisp.
3. Remove from the oven and stir with lemon zest in a mixing basin. As the chickpeas cool, they will crisp up even more.

Dressing And Salad:
1. Preheat the grill to medium heat. To make the dressing, purée all dressing ingredients in a small blender or food processor until smooth, adding 1 tablespoon water at a time to modify consistency and seasoning with salt and pepper to taste. Set aside the dressing.
2. To make the salad, follow these steps: 1 ½ tablespoons oil, brushed on the bread, 1 tablespoon oil, ¼ teaspoon salt, and ¼ teaspoon pepper, brushed on onion slices Season radishes with a pinch of salt and the remaining ½ tbsp oil. Using small skewers, thread radishes. 2 to 3 minutes per side on the grill, until toasted; immediately massage with garlic. Onions and radishes should be grilled until soft, about 5 minutes per side for onions and 6–8 minutes for radishes.
3. Separate the onion rings and tear the bread into pieces. Toss half of the dressing with the lettuce to coat it. Fold in the grilled croutons and onion rings gently. Serve with radish skewers, crispy chickpeas, and any leftover dressing for dipping or drizzling.

Nutrition:
Calories: 70 Carbohydrates: 5.8g Fiber: 1g Proteins: 2.9g

119. Steak and Mushroom Noodles

Preparation time: 10 minutes **Cooking time:** 12 minutes Servings: 4

Ingredients:
- 100g shiitake mushrooms, halved, if large
- 100g chestnut mushrooms, sliced
- 150g udon noodles
- 75g kale, finely chopped
- 75g baby leaf spinach, chopped
- 2 sirloin steaks
- 2 teaspoons miso paste
- 2.5cm piece fresh ginger, finely chopped
- 1 star anise
- 1 red chili, finely sliced
- 1 red onion, finely chopped
- 1 fresh coriander (cilantro) chopped
- 1 liter (1½ pints) warm water

Directions:
1. Spill the water into a saucepan and add in the miso, star anise, and ginger. Bring it to the boil, reduce the heat, and simmer gently. In the meantime, cook the noodles then drain them.
2. Warmth the oil in a saucepan, add the steak and cook for around 2-3 minutes on each side. Remove the meat and set aside.
3. Place the mushrooms, spinach, coriander (cilantro), and kale into the miso broth and cook for 5 minutes.
4. Warmth the remaining oil in a separate pan and fry the chili and onion for 4 minutes, until softened.
5. Serve the noodles into bowls and pour the soup on top.
6. Thinly slice the steaks and add them to the top. Serve immediately.

Nutrition:
Calories: 296 Carbohydrates: 24g Fat: 13g Proteins: 32

120. Masala Scallops

Preparation time: 10 minutes **Cooking time:** 20 minutes Servings: 4

Ingredients:
- 2 jalapenos, chopped
- 1 pound sea scallops
- A pinch of salt and black pepper
- ¼ teaspoon cinnamon powder
- 1 teaspoon garam masala
- 1 teaspoon coriander, ground
- 1 teaspoon cumin, ground
- 2 tablespoons cilantro

Directions:
1. Warmth up a pan with the oil over medium heat, add the jalapenos, cinnamon, and the other ingredients except for the scallops and cook for 10 minutes.

Nutrition:
Calories: 251 Fat: 4g Carbohydrates: 11g Proteins: 17g

121. Lemongrass and Ginger Mackerel

Preparation time: 10 minutes **Cooking time:** 25 minutes Servings: 4

Ingredients:
- 4 mackerel filets, skinless and boneless
- 1 tablespoon ginger, grated
- 2 lemongrass sticks, chopped
- 2 red chilies, chopped
- Juice of 1 lime
- A handful parsley, chopped

Directions:
1. In a roasting pan, combine the mackerel with the oil, ginger, and the other ingredients, toss and bake at 390F for 25 minutes.
2. Divide everything between plates and serve.

Nutrition:
Calories: 251 Fat: 3g Carbohydrates: 14g Proteins: 8g

122. Mashed Potatoes

Preparation time: 10 minutes Cooking time: 10 minutes Servings: 2

Ingredients:
- 4 potatoes, halved
- ¼ tablespoons chives, chopped

- 1 teaspoon minced garlic
- ¾ teaspoon sea salt
- 2 tablespoons butter, unsalted
- ¼ teaspoon ground black pepper

Directions:
1. Take a medium pot, place it over medium-high heat, add potatoes, cover with water and boil until cooked and tender.
2. When done, drain the potatoes, let them cool for 10 minutes, peel them and return them to the pot.
3. Mash the potatoes by using a hand mixer until fluffy, add remaining ingredients except for chives, and then stir until mixed.
4. Sprinkle chives over the top and then serve.

Nutrition:
Calories:396 Fat: 5g Carbohydrates: 10g Proteins: 23g

123. Quinoa with Vegetables

Preparation time: 10 minutes   **Cooking time:** 5 to 6 hours   Servings: 8

Ingredients:
- 2 cups quinoa, rinsed and drained
- 2 onions, chopped
- 2 carrots, peeled and sliced
- 1 cup sliced cremini mushrooms
- 3 garlic cloves, minced
- 4 cups low-sodium vegetable broth
- ½ teaspoon salt
- 1 teaspoon dried marjoram leaves
- ⅛ teaspoon freshly ground black pepper

Directions:
1. In a 6-quart slow cooker, mix all the ingredients.
2. Cover and cook on low heat for 5 to 6 hours, or until the quinoa and vegetables are tender.
3. Stir the mixture and serve.

Nutrition:
Calories: 204 Carbohydrates: 35g Fiber: 4g Fat: 3g Proteins: 7g

124. Cold Cauliflower-Coconut Soup

Preparation time: 7 minutes   **Cooking time:** 10 minutes   Servings: 3-4

Ingredients:
- 1 pound (450g) new cauliflower
- 1 ¼ cup (300ml) unsweetened coconut milk
- 1 cup of water (best: antacid water)
- 2 tbsp. new lime juice
- ⅓ cup cold squeezed additional virgin olive oil
- 1 cup new coriander leaves, slashed
- Spot of salt and cayenne pepper
- 1 bunch of unsweetened coconut chips

Directions:
1. Steam cauliflower for around 10 minutes.
2. At that point, set up the cauliflower with coconut milk and water in a food processor and get it started until extremely smooth.
3. Include new lime squeeze, salt and pepper, a large portion of the cleaved coriander, and the oil and blend for an additional couple of moments.
4. Pour in soup bowls and embellishment with coriander and coconut chips. Appreciate!

Nutrition:
Calories: 190 Fat: 1g Carbohydrates: 21g Proteins: 6g

125. Lettuce Bean Burritos

Preparation time: 10 minutes   Cooking time: 0 minutes   Servings: 4

Ingredients:
- 1 can white beans
- Head of romaine lettuce
- 1 red onion
- ½ cup basil
- 1 organic tomato
- 2 tbsp. lemon juice
- Himalayan pink salt
- Black pepper

Directions:

1. Rinse and drain the beans.
2. Pull off 8 of the largest lettuce leaves and chop the hard stem off the bottom and set aside. Finely chop the onion and basil. Core and dice the tomato.
3. Mix the beans, onion, tomato, basil, lemon juice, and a pinch of salt and pepper.
4. To shape the wraps, spread a spoonful of the white bean mix down the middle of each lettuce leaf and roll the leaf like a burrito.
5. Se seam-side down on a platter and serve.

Nutrition:

Calories: 244 Fat: 2g Proteins: 11g Carbohydrates: 50g Fiber: 10g

126. Mango Chutney Wraps

Preparation time: 10 minutes Cooking time: 3 minutes Servings: 8

Ingredients:
- 3 ripe mangoes
- 1 avocado
- 4 tbsp. lime juice
- 2 tbsp. coconut oil
- 2 tbsp. tahini
- 1 tsp. chili flakes
- ½ cup coriander leaves
- Sea salt
- 1 tbsp. fresh ginger
- 16 sheets of rice paper
- 3 carrots
- 2 bell peppers
- 1 cucumber
- Black pepper

Directions:
1. Set the mango meat and cut the avocado in half, dash the pit, and scoop out the flesh.
2. Add the mango flesh of 2 mangos to a blender along with the avocado, 2 tbsp. lime juice, oil, tahini, chili, coriander leaves, and a pinch of salt.
3. Slice the ginger before adding to the blender. Pulse then blend until smooth.
4. Pour the blended mango into a bowl and refrigerate until serving.
5. Chop the remaining mango flesh into slices.
6. To prepare the wraps, carefully dip the rice paper into hot water for no more than 10 seconds, then lay them flat and let dry for 2 minutes.
7. While you wait, thinly slice your carrots, peppers, and cucumber.
8. After the wraps have dried, spread a tbsp. of mango dip down the middle of each sheet of rice paper. Put the dried mango slices and vegetable slices in the middle. Dribble some lime juice on top and a smidge of salt and pepper, then roll up like a burrito.
9. Serve with more mango dip on the side!

Nutrition:

Calories: 362 Fat: 13g Carbohydrates: 52.5g Fiber: 3g Proteins: 8g

127. Chickpea Fajitas

Preparation time: 10 minutes Cooking time: 30 minutes Servings: 4

Ingredients:
- For the Chickpea Fajitas:
- 1 ½ cups cooked chickpeas
- 1 medium white onion, peeled, sliced
- 2 medium green bell peppers, cored, sliced
- 1 tablespoon fajita seasoning
- 2 tablespoons olive oil

For the Cream:
- ½ cup cashews, soaked
- 1 clove of garlic, peeled
- ½ teaspoon salt
- ½ teaspoon ground cumin
- ¼ cup lime juice
- ¼ cup water
- 1 tablespoon olive oil

To serve:
- Sliced avocado for topping
- Chopped lettuce for topping
- 4 flour tortillas
- Chopped tomatoes for topping

- Salsa for topping
- Chopped cilantro for topping

Directions:
1. Prepare chickpeas and for this, whisk together seasoning and oil until combined, add onion, pepper, and chickpeas, toss until well coated, then spread them in a baking sheet and roast for 30 minutes at 400F until crispy and browned, stirring halfway.
2. Meanwhile, prepare the cream and for this, place all its ingredients in a food processor and pulse until smooth, set aside until required.
3. When chickpeas and vegetables have roasted, top them evenly on tortillas, then top them evenly with avocado, lettuce, tomatoes, salsa, and cilantro and serve.

Nutrition:
Calories: 300 Carbohydrates: 46g Proteins: 5.3g Fat: 10.6g

128. Garlic and White Bean Soup

Preparation time: 15 minutes   Cooking time: 16 minutes   Servings: 4

Ingredients:
- 45 ounces cooked cannellini beans
- ¼ teaspoon dried thyme
- 2 teaspoons minced garlic
- ⅛ teaspoon crushed red pepper
- ½ teaspoon dried rosemary
- ⅛ teaspoon ground black pepper
- 2 tablespoons olive oil
- 4 cups vegetable broth

Directions:
1. Place one-third of white beans in a food processor, then pour in 2 cups broth and pulse for 2 minutes until smooth.
2. Set a pot over medium heat, attach oil and when hot, add garlic and cook for 1 minute until fragrant. Add pureed beans into the pan along with remaining beans, sprinkle with spices and herbs, pour in the broth, stir until combined, and bring the mixture to boil over medium-high heat.
3. Switch heat to medium-low level, simmer the beans for 15 minutes, and then mash them with a fork. Taste the soup to adjust seasoning and then serve.

Nutrition:
Calories: 221 Fat: 2g Carbohydrates: 1g Proteins: 3g

129. Quinoa and Chickpeas Salad

Preparation time: 10 minutes   Cooking time: 0 minute   Servings: 4

Ingredients:
- ¾ cup chopped broccoli
- ½ cup quinoa, cooked
- 15 ounces cooked chickpeas
- ½ teaspoon minced garlic
- ⅓ teaspoon ground black pepper
- ⅔ teaspoon salt
- 1 teaspoon dried tarragon
- 2 teaspoons mustard
- 1 tablespoon lemon juice
- 3 tablespoons olive oil

Directions:
1. Take a large bowl, place all the ingredients in it, and stir until well combined. Serve straight away.

Nutrition:
Calories: 311 Fat: 2g Carbohydrates: 64g Fiber: 13g Proteins: 11g

130. Pecan Rice

Preparation time: 5 minutes   Cooking time: 7 minutes   Servings: 4

Ingredients:
- ¼ cup chopped white onion
- ¼ teaspoon ground ginger
- ½ cup chopped pecans
- ¼ teaspoon salt
- 2 tablespoons minced parsley
- ¼ teaspoon ground black pepper
- ¼ teaspoon dried basil
- 2 tablespoons vegan margarine
- 1 cup brown rice, cooked

Directions:
1. Take a skillet pan, place it over medium heat, add margarine and when it melts, add all the ingredients except for rice and stir until mixed.
2. Cook for 5 minutes, then stir in rice until combined and continue cooking for 2 minutes.
3. Serve straight away

Nutrition:
Calories: 432 Fat: 12g Carbohydrates: 6g Proteins: 4g

131. Barley Bake

Preparation time: 10 minutes Cooking time: 96 minutes Servings: 6

Ingredients:
- 1 cup pearl barley
- 1 medium white onion, peeled, diced
- 2 green onions, sliced
- ½ cup sliced mushrooms
- ⅛ teaspoon ground black pepper
- ¼ teaspoon salt
- ½ cup chopped parsley
- ½ cup pine nuts
- ¼ cup vegan butter
- 29 ounces vegetable broth

Directions:
1. Place a skillet pan over medium-high heat, add butter and when it melts, stir in onion and barley, add nuts and cook for 5 minutes until light brown.
2. Add mushrooms, green onions and parsley, sprinkle with salt and black pepper, cook for 1 minute and then transfer the mixture into a casserole dish.
3. Pour in broth, stir until mixed and bake for 90 minutes until barley is tender and has absorbed all the liquid.
4. Serve straight away

Nutrition:
Calories: 126 Fat: 4g Carbohydrates: 4g Proteins: 13g

132. Black Beans, Corn, and Yellow Rice

Preparation time: 10 minutes Cooking time: 25 minutes Servings: 8

Ingredients:
- 8 ounces yellow rice mix
- 15.25 ounces cooked kernel corn
- 1 ¼ cups water
- 15 ounces cooked black beans
- 1 teaspoon ground cumin
- 2 teaspoons lime juice
- 2 tablespoons olive oil

Directions:
1. Place a saucepan over high heat, add oil, water, and rice, bring the mixture to a bowl, and then switch heat to medium-low level.
2. Par boil for 25 minutes until rice is tender and all the liquid has been absorbed and then set the rice to a large bowl.
3. Add remaining ingredients into the rice, stir until mixed and serve straight away

Nutrition:
Calories: 178 Fat: 8.1g Carbohydrates: 21.3g Proteins: 3.9g Fiber: 5.2g

133. Black Beans and Rice

Preparation time: 10 minutes Cooking time: 28 minutes Servings: 4

Ingredients:
- ¾ cup white rice
- 1 medium white onion, peeled, chopped
- 3 ½ cups cooked black beans
- 1 teaspoon minced garlic
- ¼ teaspoon cayenne pepper
- 1 teaspoon ground cumin
- 1 teaspoon olive oil
- 1 ½ cups vegetable broth

Directions:
1. Take a large pot over medium-high heat, add oil and when hot, add onion and garlic and cook for 4 minutes until sauté.

2. Then stir in rice, cook for 2 minutes, pour in the broth, bring it to a boil, switch heat to the low level and cook for 20 minutes until tender.
3. Stir in remaining ingredients, cook for 2 minutes, and then serve straight away.

Nutrition:
Calories: 240 Fat: 0g Proteins: 0g Carbohydrates: 48g Fiber: 16g

134. Vegetable and Chickpea Loaf

Preparation time: 10 minutes   Cooking time: 15 minutes   Servings: 4

Ingredients:
- 1 tsp. Salt
- 3.5tsp. Dried sage
- 1tsp. Dried savory
- 1tbsp. Soy sauce
- 3.25cup Parsley
- 4.5cup Breadcrumbs
- 1.75cup Oats 1.75
- 2.75cup Chickpea flour
- 1.5cup cooked chickpeas
- 2Minced garlic cloves
- 1Chopped yellow onion
- 1Shredded carrot
- 1Shredded white potato

Directions:
1. Set the oven to 350F. Take out a loaf pan and then grease it up.
2. Squeeze out the liquid from the potato and add to the food processor with garlic, onion, and carrot.
3. Add the chickpeas and pulse to blend well. Add in the rest of the ingredients here, and when it is done, use your hands to form this into a loaf and add to the pan.
4. Place into the oven to bake for a bit until it is nice and firm. Let it cool down and then slice.

Nutrition:
Calories: 351 Proteins: 16.86g Fat: 6.51g Carbohydrates: 64g

135. Thyme and Lemon Couscous

Preparation time: 5 minutes   Cooking time: 10 minutes   Servings: 4

Ingredients:
- 3.25cup Chopped parsley
- 1.5cup Couscous
- 2tbsp. Chopped thyme
- Juice and zest of a lemon
- 2.75cup Vegetable stock

Directions:
1. Take out a pot and add in the thyme, lemon juice, and vegetable stock. Stir in the couscous after it has gotten to a boil and then take off the heat.
2. Allow sitting covered until it can take in all the liquid. Then fluff up with a form.
3. Swirl in the parsley and lemon zest, then serve warm.

Nutrition:
Calories: 922 Proteins: 2.7g Fat: 101.04g Carbohydrates: 10.02g

136. Pesto and White Bean Pasta

Preparation time: 10 minutes   Cooking time: 10 minutes   Servings: 4

Ingredients:
- 2.5cup Chopped black olives
- 2.25Diced red onion
- 1cup Chopped tomato
- 2.5cup Spinach pesto
- 1.5cup Cannellini beans
- 8oz. Rotini pasta, cooked

Directions:
1. Bring out a bowl and toss together the pesto, beans, and pasta.
2. Add in the olives, red onion, and tomato, and toss around a bit more before serving.

Nutrition:
Calories: 544 Carbohydrates: 83g Fat: 17g Proteins: 23g

137. Baked Okra and Tomato

Preparation time: 10 minutes   Cooking time: 75 minutes   Servings: 2

Ingredients:
- ½cup lima beans, frozen
- 4 tomatoes, chopped
- 8ounces okra, fresh and washed, stemmed, sliced into ½ inch thick slices
- 1onion, sliced into rings
- ½sweet pepper, seeded and sliced thin
- Pinch of crushed red pepper
- Salt to taste

Directions:
1. Preheat your oven to 350 degrees Fahrenheit
2. Cook lima beans in water accordingly and drain them, take a 2quart casserole tin
3. Add all listed ingredients to the dish and cover with foil, bake for 45 minutes
4. Uncover the dish, stir well and bake for 35 more minutes
5. Stir then serve and enjoy!

Nutrition:
Calories: 55 Fat: 0g Carbohydrates: 12g Proteins: 3g

138. Bean and Carrot Spirals

Preparation time: 10 minutes   Cooking time: 40 minutes   Servings: 2

Ingredients:
- 4 8-inch flour tortillas
- 1 ½cups of Easy Mean White Bean dip
- 10 ounces spinach leaves
- ½ cup diced carrots
- ½ cup diced red peppers

Directions:
1. Start by preparing the bean dip, seen above. Next, spread out the bean dip on each tortilla, making sure to leave about a ¾ inch white border on the tortillas' surface. Next, place spinach in the center of the tortilla, followed by carrots and red peppers.
2. Roll the tortillas into tight rolls and cover every roll with plastic wrap or aluminum foil.
3. Let them chill in the fridge for twenty-four hours.
4. Afterward, remove the wrap from the spirals and remove the very ends of the rolls. Slice the rolls into six individual spiral pieces and arrange them on a platter for serving. Enjoy!

Nutrition:
Calories: 205 Proteins: 6.41g Fat: 4.16g Carbohydrates: 5.13g

139. Tofu Nuggets with Barbecue Glaze

Preparation time: 10 minutes   Cooking time: 25 minutes   Servings: 2

Ingredients:
- 32 ounces tofu
- 1 cup quick vegan barbecue sauce

Directions:
1. Set the oven to 425F.
2. Next, slice the tofu and blot the tofu with clean towels. Next, slice and dice the tofu and eliminate the water from the tofu material.
3. Stir the tofu with the vegan barbecue sauce and place the tofu on a baking sheet.
4. Bake the tofu for fifteen minutes. Afterward, stir the tofu and bake the tofu for an additional ten minutes.
5. Enjoy!

Nutrition:
Calories: 311 Proteins: 19.94g Fat: 21.02g Carbohydrates: 15.55g

140. Peppered Pinto Beans

Preparation time: 10 minutes   Cooking time: 15 minutes   Servings: 4

Ingredients:
- 1tsp. Chili powder
- 1tsp. ground cumin
- 3.5cup Vegetable
- 2cans Pinto beans

- 1 Minced jalapeno
- 1 Diced red bell pepper
- 1 tsp. Olive oil

Directions:
1. Take out a pot and heat the oil. Cook the jalapeno and pepper for a bit before adding in the pepper, salt, cumin, broth, and beans.
2. Place to a boil and then reduce the heat to cook for a bit. After 10 minutes, let it cool and serve.

Nutrition:
Calories: 183 Carbohydrates: 3.2g Fat: 2g Proteins: 11g

141. Chili Fennel

Preparation time: 10 minutes Cooking time: 8 minutes Servings: 4

Ingredients:
- 2 fennel bulbs, cut into quarters
- 3 tablespoons olive oil
- Salt and black pepper to the taste
- 1 garlic clove, minced
- 1 red chili pepper, chopped
- ¾ cup veggie stock
- Juice of ½ lemon

Directions:
1. Heat a pan that fits your Air Fryer with the oil over medium-high heat, add garlic and chili pepper, stir and cook for 2 minutes.
2. Add fennel, salt, pepper, stock, and lemon juice, toss to coat, introduce in your Air Fryer and cook at 350F for at least 6 minutes.
3. Divide into plates and serve as a side dish.

Nutrition:
Calories: 158 Proteins: 3.57g Fat: 11.94g Carbohydrates: 11.33g

142. Cajun and Balsamic Okra

Preparation time: 10 minutes **Cooking time:** 15 minutes Servings: 2

Ingredients:
- 1 cup okra, sliced
- ½ cup crushed tomatoes
- 1 teaspoon Cajun seasoning
- 2 tablespoons balsamic vinegar
- 1 teaspoon salt
- 1 teaspoon ground black pepper
- 1 tablespoon fresh parsley, chopped
- 1 teaspoon olive oil

Directions:
1. Warmth up a pan with the oil over medium heat, add the okra, seasoning, and the remaining ingredients, toss and cook for 15 minutes.
2. Divide into bowls and serve.

Nutrition:
Calories: 162 Fat: 4.5g Fiber: 4.6g Carbohydrates: 12.6g Proteins: 3g

143. Cashew Zucchinis

Preparation time: 10 minutes **Cooking time:** 40 minutes Servings: 4

Ingredients:
- 1 pound zucchinis, sliced
- ½ cup cashews, soaked and drained
- 1 cup coconut milk
- ¼ teaspoon nutmeg, ground
- 1 teaspoon chili powder
- A pinch of salt and black pepper

Directions:
1. In a roasting pan, mix the zucchinis with the cashews and the other ingredients, toss gently, and cook at 380 degrees F for 40 minutes.
2. Divide into bowls and serve.

Nutrition:
Calories: 200 Fat: 5g Fiber: 3g Carbohydrates: 7.1g Proteins: 6g

144. Cauliflower Gnocchi

Preparation time: 10 minutes **Cooking time:** 40 minutes Servings: 4

Ingredients:
- 3 pounds of cauliflower florets
- 2 cups of marinara sauce or 2 cups of quartered tomatoes without skin
- 1 cup of whole-wheat flour
- 1 teaspoon of sea salt
- Basil, for garnishing

Cashew Cheese:
- 1 cup of raw cashews (soaked for hours)
- 1-2 tablespoons of apple cider vinegar
- 2-4 tablespoons of water
- ½ teaspoon of salt
- optional additions: smoked paprika, nutritional yeast, fresh or dried herbs, granulated garlic

Directions:
1. Set cauliflower florets in a large pot, pour water to cover them, and set it to a boil. Once boiled, parboil on low heat for 22 minutes until tender. Drain and set to cool.
2. After cooling, squeeze out extra water: Set some of the cauliflower on a dish towel, squeeze, and transfer to a large bowl. Repeat with the remaining cauliflower.
3. Press cauliflower with a fork. Add flour and salt in the bowl, merge all ingredients well by hand, and make a dough.
4. Set flour on a work surface, divide the prepared dough into 8 equal parts. Set each piece into a rope (10 inches long and ½-inch thick) and set aside.
5. Divide each rope into 13 equal gnocchi-like pieces. If the dough becomes too sticky, scatter some flour on your hands.
6. Set a skillet on medium heat and warm. Take half of the formed gnocchi and put on the hot skillet. Let them cook for 2 minutes, then slowly flip gnocchi on another side. Sprinkle salt on the top and cook. Set aside. Redo it with the remaining part of the formed gnocchi.
7. Meanwhile, cook the cashew cheese. Set the soaked cashews in a food processor with vinegar and salt, and pulse repeatedly. Attach water by a tablespoon at a time to get the desired consistency and blend. Taste and feel free to add any optional additions.
8. Bring everything back to the skillet, pour marinara sauce (tomatoes) on the top and stir. Take out from the heat and spread the cooked cashew cheese on the top.
9. Serve and enjoy your Cauliflower Gnocchi!

Nutrition:
Calories: 228 Carbohydrates: 42.6g Proteins: 12g Fat: 2g

145. Curry Chickpea

Preparation time: 10 minutes **Cooking time:** 21 minutes Servings: 4

Ingredients:
- 1 chopped red bell pepper
- ½ chopped red onion
- 2 cups of cooked chickpeas
- 1 can of coconut milk
- ¼ cup of chopped fresh basil
- 1 tablespoon of minced fresh ginger
- 1 minced clove garlic
- 2 tablespoons of maple syrup
- 1 tablespoon of fresh lime juice
- 1 tablespoon of curry powder
- 1 teaspoon of sea salt

Directions:
1. Set a large deep skillet on medium heat, pour water, and warm it. Add chopped pepper with onion into it and sauté 5 minutes until softened.
2. Add in curry powder, garlic, and ginger. Continue cooking for 1 minute.
3. Add chickpeas, coconut milk, maple syrup, and salt to the vegetables and stir it. Set it to a boil, reduce to low heat and simmer, covered, for 15 minutes.
4. Add lime juice with basil and stir. Cook until basil is wilted, then season according to your taste.
5. Serve warm* and enjoy your Curry Chickpea!

Nutrition:
Calories: 268 Fat: 24g Carbohydrates: 14g Proteins: 3g

146. Grilled Margherita

Preparation time: 10 minutes **Cooking time:** 24 minutes Servings: 4

Ingredients:
- 1 cup of whole-wheat flour
- 1 cup of soy yogurt
- 1 ½ cups of arugula
- ¼ cup of marinara sauce
- 1 ½ teaspoons of baking powder
- ½ teaspoon of sea salt
- Black pepper, to taste

Cashew Cheese:
- 1 cup of raw cashews (soaked for 3-24 hours)
- 1-2 tablespoons of apple cider vinegar
- 2-4 tablespoons of water
- ½ teaspoon of salt
- optional additions: smoked paprika, nutritional yeast, fresh or dried herbs, granulated garlic

Directions:
1. Attach flour, salt, and baking powder into a medium mixing bowl and mix them. Pour soy yogurt and whisk it with a fork until well mixed.
2. Lightly spread some flour on your work surface and take the mixture from the bowl. Knead the dough until tacky but not sticky. It shouldn't stick to your hands.
3. Set the dough into 4 equal parts and form balls about 3 ounces each. Dust flour on the work surface and roll the dough into thin ovals using a rolling pin.
4. Preheat your grill on high heat and place the rolled dough on the grill. Cover and cook 1-1.5 minutes on each side until grill lines stay.
5. Meanwhile, cook the cashew cheese. Set the soaked cashews in a food processor with vinegar and salt, and pulse repeatedly. Attach water by a tablespoon at a time to get the desired consistency and blend. Taste and feel free to add any optional additions.
6. Spread 1 tablespoon of marinara sauce over the grilled pizza bases and sprinkle the cooked cashew cheese on the top. Grill it for 2-3 minutes. Take it out and add arugula, black pepper, and salt.
7. Repeat steps 6 and 7 with the remaining part of the dough.
8. Serve and enjoy your Grilled Margherita!

Nutrition:
Calories: 242 Carbohydrates: 29.5g Proteins: 15.5g Fat: 7g

147. Vegan Moroccan Stew

Preparation time: 10 minutes **Cooking time:** 30 minutes Servings: 4

Ingredients:
- 4 cups of cubed butternut squash
- 1 cup of cooked chickpeas
- 1 cup of green lentils
- 1 cup of chopped tomatoes
- 1 chopped white onion
- 6 minced garlic cloves
- 2 ½ cups of vegetable broth
- Juice of ½ a lemon
- ⅓ cup of chopped cilantro
- 2 teaspoons of cumin
- 1 teaspoon of ground turmeric
- 1 teaspoon of cinnamon
- ¼ teaspoon of cayenne powder
- Pinch of sea salt and black pepper

Directions:
1. Put a large pot on medium heat. Add garlic and onion, cook until softened.
2. Add in cayenne, cinnamon, turmeric, cumin and cook for 30-60 second until fragrant.
3. Add in butternut squash, chickpeas, lentils, broth, tomatoes, pepper and salt. Bring it to a boil, reduce to lower heat, cover and simmer for 20 minutes until the vegetables are fully cooked. Stir in lemon juice. Taste and add more seasonings if desired.
4. Serve warm and enjoy Vegan Moroccan Stew!

Nutrition:
Calories: 431 Proteins: 27.4g Fat: 6g Carbohydrates: 78g

148. Lime Bean Artichoke Wraps

Preparation time: 10 minutes **Cooking time:** 10 minutes Servings: 2

Ingredients:
- Lima bean spread
- 1 cup cooked baby lima beans
- 2 tablespoons nutritional yeast
- 2 tablespoons parsley, chopped
- ½ teaspoon garlic, minced
- ½ teaspoon onion powder
- 2 teaspoons fresh lime juice
- 2 teaspoons white balsamic vinegar
- Wraps
- 2 gluten-free vegan wraps
- 1 cup raw broccoli, sliced lengthwise
- 2 whole hearts of palm, sliced lengthwise

Directions:
1. Blend lime beans with yeast, parsley, garlic, onion powder, lime juice and vinegar in a blender until smooth.
2. Spread the bean mixture on top of the wraps and top them with broccoli and hearts of palm.
3. Roll the wraps like a burrito and cut in half.
4. Grill the wraps in the grill over high heat for 5 minutes per side.
5. Serve.

Nutrition:
Calories: 432 Fat: 12g Carbohydrates: 6g Proteins: 4g

149. Butternut Squash Lasagna

Preparation time: 10 minutes **Cooking time:** 1 hour 30 minutes Servings: 6

Ingredients:
- 2 tablespoons olive oil
- 2 pounds butternut squash, cubed
- ½ cup water
- 4 amaretti cookies, crumbled
- 8 ounces shiitake mushrooms, sliced
- ¼ cup butter
- ¼ cup whole-wheat flour
- 3½ cups almond milk
- ½ teaspoon ground nutmeg
- 1 cup fresh basil leaves
- 13 ounces DeLillo no-boil lasagna noodles
- 3 cups vegan cheese, shredded
- Salt and black pepper, to taste

Directions:
1. Preheat your oven to 375F.
2. Sauté squash with black pepper, salt and oil in a skillet for 5 minutes.
3. Add water to the squash, cover and cook for about 20 minutes on medium heat. Blend the squash with amaretti in a blender until smooth. Sauté mushrooms with oil and ¼ teaspoons salt in a skillet for 10 minutes. Mix butter with flour in a skillet for 1 minute.
4. Pour in milk, mix well until lump-free then boil the mixture.
5. Stir in black pepper, nutmeg and ¼ teaspoons salt. Mix well then cook for about 5 minutes until the sauce thickens. Add basil and blend well with a blender.
6. Grease a 13x9 -inch baking dish with butter.
7. Spread ¾ cup sauce in the baking dish. Arrange the lasagna noodles at the bottom of this dish.
8. Top the noodles with ⅓ squash puree and add ⅓ mushrooms on top.
9. Drizzle 1 cup vegan cheese on top.
10. Repeat all the layers and cover this dish with a foil sheet.
11. Bake the prepared lasagna for 40 minutes in the oven.
12. Remove the tin foil from the top and bake for another 15 minutes.
13. Serve warm.

Nutrition:
Calories: 240 Fat: 0g Proteins: 0g Carbohydrates: 48g Fiber: 16g

150. Broccoli Dip

Preparation time: 10 minutes **Cooking time:** 25 minutes Servings: 2

Ingredients:
- 1 cup white beans, drained
- 1 cup cashews, soaked
- 1 tablespoon lemon juice
- 1 tablespoon tapioca starch
- 2 tablespoons nutritional yeast
- 1 teaspoon garlic powder
- 1 teaspoon onion powder
- ½ teaspoon paprika
- Salt, to taste
- 1 pinch red pepper flakes
- 1¼ cup almond milk
- 1½ cups fresh broccoli, florets

Directions:
1. At 375 F, preheat your oven.
2. Spread broccoli in a baking sheet.
3. Blend rest of the dip ingredients in a blender until smooth.
4. Spread this mixture over the broccoli and bake for 25 minutes.
5. Serve.

Nutrition:
Calories: 455 Carbohydrates: 28g Fat: 9.8g Proteins: 20g

Snack

### 151.	Smoky Red Pepper Hummus

Preparation time: 5 minutes	Cooking time: 0 minutes	Servings: 1 ½ cup

Ingredients:
- ¼ cup roasted red peppers
- 1 cup cooked chickpeas
- ⅛ teaspoon garlic powder
- ½ teaspoon salt
- ⅛ teaspoon ground black pepper
- ¼ teaspoon ground cumin
- ¼ teaspoon red chili powder
- 1 tablespoon Tahini
- 2 tablespoons water

Directions:
1. Set all the ingredients in the jar of the food processor and then pulse until smooth.
2. Tip the hummus in a bowl and then serve with vegetable slices.

Nutrition:
Calories: 489 Fat: 30g Proteins: 9g Carbohydrates: 15g Fiber: 6g

### 152.	Roasted Tamari Almonds

Preparation time: 5 minutes	**Cooking time:** 10-15 minutes	Servings: 8

Ingredients:
- 1 pound (454 g) raw almonds
- 3 tablespoons tamari
- 1 tablespoon nutritional yeast
- 1 to 2 teaspoons chili powder

Directions:
1. Preheat the oven to 400F (205C). Set a large baking tray with parchment paper and set aside.
2. Mix the almonds and tamari in a medium bowl and toss to coat.
3. Arrange the almonds on the prepared baking tray in a single layer.

4. Roast in the preheated oven until browned, about 10 to 15 minutes. Set the almonds halfway through the cooking time.
5. Let the almonds cool for 10 minutes in the baking tray. Sprinkle it with nutritional yeast and chili powder. Serve immediately, or store in the fridge for up to 2 weeks.

Nutrition:
Calories: 91 Fat: 28.3g Carbohydrates: 13.2g Proteins: 12.2g Fiber: 7.4g

153. Tomatillo Salsa

Preparation time: 5 minutes   Cooking time: 15 minutes   Servings: 2 cups

Ingredients:
- 5 medium tomatillos, chopped
- 3 cloves of garlic, peeled, chopped
- 3 Roma tomatoes, chopped
- 1 jalapeno, chopped
- ½ of a red onion, peeled, chopped
- 1 Anaheim chili
- 2 teaspoons salt
- 1 teaspoon ground cumin
- 1 lime, juiced
- ¼ cup cilantro leaves
- ¾ cup of water

Directions:
1. Take a medium pot, place it over medium heat, pour in water, and then add onion, tomatoes, tomatillo, jalapeno, and Anaheim chili.
2. Sauté the vegetables for 15 minutes, remove the pot from heat, add cilantro and lime juice and then stir in salt.
3. Remove pot from heat and then pulse by using an immersion blender until smooth.
4. Serve the salsa with chips.

Nutrition:
Calories: 317.4 Fat: 0g Proteins: 16g Carbohydrates: 64g Fiber: 16g

154. Arugula Pesto Couscous

Preparation time: 10 minutes   Cooking time: 16 minutes   Servings: 4

Ingredients:
- 8 ounces Israeli couscous
- 3 large tomatoes, chopped
- 3 cups arugula leaves
- ½ cup parsley leaves
- 6 cloves of garlic, peeled
- ½ cup walnuts
- ¾ teaspoon salt
- 1 cup and 1 tablespoon olive oil
- 2 cups vegetable broth

Directions:
1. Take a medium saucepan, place it over medium-high heat, add 1 tablespoon of oil and then let it heat.
2. Add couscous, stir until mixed, and then cook for 4 minutes until fragrant and toasted.
3. Pour in the broth, stir until mixed, bring it to a boil, switch heat to medium level and then simmer for 12 minutes until the couscous has absorbed all the liquid and turn tender.
4. When done, remove the pan from heat, fluff it with a fork, and then set aside until required.
5. While couscous cooks, prepare the pesto, and for this, place walnuts in a blender, add garlic, and then pulse until nuts have broken.
6. Add arugula, parsley, and salt, pulse until well combined, and then blend in oil until smooth.
7. Transfer couscous to a salad bowl, add tomatoes and prepared pesto, and then toss until mixed.
8. Serve straight away.

Nutrition:
Calories: 73 Fat: 4g Proteins: 2g Carbohydrates: 8g Fiber: 2g

155. Oatmeal and Raisin Balls

Preparation time: 40 minutes   Cooking time: 0 minutes   **Servings:** 12 balls

Ingredients:
- 1 cup rolled oats
- ¼ cup raisins

- ½ cup peanut butter

Directions:
1. Place oats in a large bowl, add raisins and peanut butter, and then stir until well combined.
2. Shape the mixture into twelve balls, 1 tablespoon of mixture per ball, and then arrange the balls on a baking sheet.
3. Bring the baking sheet into the freezer for 30 minutes until firm and then serve.

Nutrition:
Calories: 135 Fat: 6g Proteins: 8g Carbohydrates: 13g Fiber: 4g

156. Oat Crunch Apple Crisp

Preparation time: 10 minutes   Cooking time: 35 minutes   Servings: 6

Ingredients:
- 3 medium apples, cored and cut into ¼inch pieces
- ¾ cup apple juice
- 1 teaspoon vanilla extract
- 1 teaspoon ground cinnamon, divided
- 2 cups rolled oats
- ¼ cup maple syrup

Directions:
1. Warmth the oven to 375F
2. In a large bowl, merge the apple slices, apple juice, vanilla, and ½ teaspoon of cinnamon. Mix well to thoroughly coat the apple slices.
3. Layer the apple slices on the bottom of a round or square baking dish. Take any leftover liquid and pour it over the apple slices.
4. In a large bowl, stir together the oats, maple syrup, and the remaining ½ teaspoon of cinnamon until the oats are completely coated.
5. Sprinkle the oat mixture over the apples, being sure to spread it out evenly so that none of the apple slices are visible.
6. Bake for 35 minutes, or until the oats begin to turn golden brown, and serve.

Nutrition:
Calories: 150 Fat: 1.0g Carbohydrates: 25.9g Proteins: 17.1g Fiber: 2.0

157. Pico de Gallo

Preparation time: 5 minutes   Cooking time: 0 minutes   Servings: 3

Ingredients:
- ½ of a medium red onion
- 2 cups diced tomato
- ½ cup chopped cilantro
- 1 jalapeno pepper, minced
- ⅛ teaspoon salt
- ¼ teaspoon ground black pepper
- ½ of a lime, juiced
- 1 teaspoon olive oil

Directions:
1. Take a large bowl, place all the ingredients in it and then stir until well mixed.
2. Serve the Pico de Gallo with chips.

Nutrition:
Calories: 790 Fat: 6.4g Proteins: 25.6g Carbohydrates: 195.2g Fiber: 35.2g

158. Beet Balls

Preparation time: 10 minutes   Cooking time: 0 minutes   Servings: 18

Ingredients:
- ½ cup oats
- 1 medium beet, cooked
- ½ cup almond flour
- ⅓ cup shredded coconut and more for coating
- ¾ cup Medjool dates, pitted
- 1 tablespoon cocoa powder
- ½ cup peanuts
- ¼ cup chocolate chips, unsweetened

Directions:
1. Place cooked beets in a blender and then pulse until chopped into very small pieces.

2. Add remaining ingredients and then pulse until the dough comes together.
3. Shape the dough into eighteen balls, coat them in some more coconut and then serve.

Nutrition:
Calories: 114.2 Fat: 2.4g Proteins: 5g Carbohydrates: 19.6g Fiber: 4.9g

159. Cheesy Crackers

Preparation time: 10 minutes   Cooking time: 15 to 20 minutes   Servings: 3

Ingredients:
- 1 ¾ cup almond meal
- 3 tablespoons nutritional yeast
- ½ teaspoon of sea salt
- 2 tablespoons lemon juice
- 1 tablespoon melted coconut oil
- 1 tablespoon ground flaxseed
- 2 ½ tablespoons water

Directions:
1. Switch on the oven, then set it to 350 degrees F and let it preheat.
2. Meanwhile, take a medium bowl, place flaxseed in it, stir in water, and then let the mixture rest for 5 minutes until thickened.
3. Place almond meal in a medium bowl, add salt and yeast and then stir until mixed.
4. Add lemon juice and oil into the flaxseed mixture and then whisk until mixed.
5. Pour the flaxseed mixture into the almond meal mixture and then stir until dough comes together.
6. Place a piece of wax paper on a clean working space, place the dough on it, secure with another piece of wax paper, and then roll dough into a ⅛-inch thick crust.
7. Cut the dough into a square shape, sprinkle salt over the top and then bake for 15 to 20 minutes until done.
8. Serve straight away.

Nutrition:
Calories: 30 Fat: 1g Proteins: 1g Carbohydrates: 5g Fiber: 0g

160. Chocolate Protein Bites

Preparation time: 10 Minutes   Cooking time: 0 Minutes   Servings: 12

Ingredients:
- ½ cup Chocolate Protein Powder
- 1 Avocado, medium
- 1 tbsp. Chocolate Chips
- 1 tbsp. Almond Butter
- 1 tbsp. Cocoa Powder
- 1 tsp. Vanilla Extract
- Dash of Salt

Directions:
1. Begin by blending avocado, almond butter, vanilla extract, and salt in a high-speed blender until you get a smooth mixture.
2. Next, spoon in the protein powder, cocoa powder, and chocolate chips to the blender.
3. Blend again until you get a smooth dough-like consistency mixture.
4. Now, check for seasoning and add more sweetness if needed.
5. Finally, with the help of a scooper, scoop out dough to make small balls.

Nutrition:
Calories: 46 Proteins: 2g Carbohydrates: 2g Fat: 2g

161. Crunchy Granola

Preparation time: 10 Minutes   Cooking time: 20 Minutes   Servings: 1

Ingredients:
- ½ cup Oats
- Dash of Salt
- 2 tbsp. Vegetable Oil
- 3 tbsp. Maple Syrup
- ⅓ cup Apple Cider Vinegar
- ½ cup Almonds
- 1 tsp. Cardamom, grounded

Directions:
1. Preheat the oven to 375F.
2. After that, mix oats, pistachios, salt, and cardamom in a large bowl.
3. Next, spoon in the vegetable oil and maple syrup to the mixture.
4. Then, transfer the mixture to a parchment-paper-lined baking sheet.
5. Bake them for 13 minutes until the mixture is toasted. Tip: Check on them now and then. Spread it out well.
6. Return the sheet to the oven for further ten minutes.
7. Detach the sheet from the oven and allow it to cool completely.
8. Serve and enjoy.

Nutrition:
Calories: 763 Proteins: 12.9g Carbohydrates: 64.8g Fat: 52.4g

162. Chocolate Almond Bars

Preparation time: 10 Minutes   Cooking time: 20 Minutes   Servings: 12

Ingredients:
- 1 cup Almonds
- 1 ½ cup Rolled Oats
- ⅓ cup Maple Syrup
- ¼ tsp. Sea Salt
- 5 oz. Protein Powder
- 1 tsp. Cinnamon

Directions:
1. For making these delicious vegan bars, you first need to place ¾ cup of the almonds and salt in the food processor.
2. Process them for a minute or until you get them in the form of almond butter.
3. Now, swirl in the rest of the ingredients to the processor and process them again until smooth.
4. Next, transfer the mixture to a greased parchment paper-lined baking sheet and spread it across evenly.
5. Press them slightly down with the back of the spoon.
6. Chop down the remaining ¼ cup of the almonds and top it across the mixture.
7. Finally, place them in the refrigerator for 20 minutes or until set.

Nutrition:
Calories: 166 Proteins: 12.8g Carbohydrates: 17.6g Fat: 6g

163. Spicy Nut and Seed Snack Mix

Preparation time: 5 Minutes   Cooking time: 5 Minutes   Servings: 4

Ingredients:
- ¼ tsp. garlic powder
- ¼ tsp. nutritional yeast
- ½ tsp. smoked paprika
- ¼ tsp. sea salt
- ¼ tsp. dried parsley
- ½ cup slivered almonds
- ½ cup cashew pieces
- ½ cup sunflower seeds
- ½ cup pepitas

Directions:
1. In a small bowl, merge the garlic powder, nutritional yeast, paprika, salt, and parsley. Set aside.
2. In a large skillet, add the almonds, cashews, sunflower seeds, pepitas and heat over low heat until warm and glistening, 3 minutes.
3. Set the heat off and stir in the parsley mixture.
4. Allow complete cooling and enjoy!

Nutrition:
Calories: 385 Proteins: 12g Carbohydrates: 16g Fat: 33g

164. Flax Crackers

Preparation time: 5 Minutes   **Cooking time:** 1 hour 30 Minutes   Servings: 4 to 6

Ingredients:
- 1 cup Flax Seeds, whole
- 2 cups Water

- ¾ cup Flaxseeds, grounded
- 1 tsp. Sea Salt
- ½ cup Chia Seeds
- 1 tsp. Black Pepper
- ½ cup Sunflower Seeds

Directions:
1. First, place all the ingredients in a large mixing bowl and mix them well. Soak them for 10 to 15 minutes.
2. After that, transfer the mixture to a parchment paper-lined baking sheet and spread it evenly. Tip: Make sure the paper lines the edges as well.
3. Next, bake it for 60 minutes at 350F.
4. Once the time is up, flip the entire bar and take off the parchment paper.
5. Bake for half an hour or until it becomes crispy and browned.
6. Allow it to cool completely and then break it down.

Nutrition:
Calories: 251 Proteins: 9.2g Carbohydrates: 14.9g Fat: 16g

165. Chocolate and Nuts Goji Bars

Preparation time: 5 Minutes   Cooking time: 0 Minutes   Servings: 4

Ingredients:
- 1 cup mixed nuts
- ¼ cup dried goji berries
- ¼ cup chopped pitted dates
- 2 tbsp. chocolate chips
- 1 ½ tsp. vanilla extract
- ¼ tsp. cinnamon powder
- 2 tbsp. vegetable oil
- 2 tbsp. golden flaxseed meal
- 1 tsp. maple syrup

Directions:
1. Attach all the ingredients to a blender and process until coarsely smooth.
2. Lay a large piece of plastic wrap on a flat surface and spread the batter on top. Bring another piece of plastic wrap on top and using a rolling pin, flatten the dough into a thick rectangle of about 1 ½ - inch thickness.
3. Remove the plastic wraps and use an oiled knife to cut the dough into bars.
4. Serve immediately and freeze any extras.

Nutrition:
Calories: 679 Proteins: 25g Carbohydrates: 11g Fat: 62g

166. Cranberry Protein Bars

Preparation time: 5 Minutes   Cooking time: 2 hours   Servings: 4

Ingredients:
- 1½ cups cashew nut butter
- 3 scoops protein powder
- 4 tbsp. butter, melted
- 1 ½ tsp. maple syrup
- ½ tsp. salt or to taste
- 4 tbsp. dried cranberries, chopped

Directions:
1. Line a medium, shallow loaf pan with baking paper and set aside.
2. In a medium bowl, merge all the ingredients and spread in the loaf pan. Refrigerate for 2 hours until the batter is firm.
3. Remove the batter from the refrigerator and turn it onto a clean, flat surface. Cut the batter into bars.
4. Serve, and freeze any extras.

Nutrition:
Calories: 968 Proteins: 29g Carbohydrates: 26g Fat: 86g

167. Onion Rings

Preparation time: 15 minutes   Cooking time: 14 minutes   Servings: 4

Ingredients:
- 1 large sweet or Vidalia onion
- ½ cup chickpea flour
- ⅓ cup unsweetened plain plant-based milk

- 2 tablespoons freshly squeezed lemon juice
- 2 tablespoons No-Salt Hot Sauce
- 1 teaspoon No-Salt Spice Blend
- ⅔ cup panko breadcrumbs

Directions:
1. Peel off and discard the top ½ inch of the root end of the sweet onion. Continue cutting the onion into ½-inch-thick slices. Carefully separate the slices into individual rings and set aside.
2. In a medium bowl, mix the chickpea flour, plant-based milk, lemon juice, hot sauce, and spice blend. Spill the breadcrumbs into a separate bowl.
3. Dip each ring into the chickpea batter so that it's completely and evenly covered. Then dip the rings into the breadcrumbs and place them in the air fryer basket.
4. Fry at 380F for 14 minutes, or until the coating is browned and crispy. Be sure to flip your onion rings over halfway through cooking. Serve warm.

Nutrition:
Calories: 127 Fat: 2g Carbohydrates: 23g Fiber: 3g Proteins: 5g

168. French Fries

Preparation time: 5 minutes Cooking time: 15 minutes Servings: 2

Ingredients:
- 1 large russet potato
- ¼ cup freshly squeezed lemon juice
- 3 tablespoons nutritional yeast
- 1 tablespoon No-Salt Spice Blend

Directions:
1. Cut the potato lengthwise into ½-inch-thick fries.
2. Pour the lemon juice onto a plate. On a second plate, mix the nutritional yeast and spice blend. Dip the fries, one at a time, into the lemon juice. Shake off the excess juice and dip the fries into the spice mixture to completely cover them on all sides. Once covered, place the fries in a single layer in the air fryer basket or on the rack.
3. Fry at 400F for 15 minutes until the fries are crispy. Shake up the basket or turn the fries over halfway through cooking. Serve immediately.

Nutrition:
Calories: 172 Fat: 0g Carbohydrates: 36g Fiber: 3g Proteins: 6g

169. Roasted Asparagus

Preparation time: 10 minutes Cooking time: 5 minutes Servings: 4

Ingredients:
- 1 tablespoon tahini
- 1 tablespoon freshly squeezed lemon juice
- 1 tablespoon water
- 1 teaspoon No-Salt Spice Blend
- 1 pound fresh asparagus, woody ends trimmed

Directions:
1. In a large bowl, merge together the tahini, lemon juice, water, and spice blend until well combined.
2. Attach the asparagus to the bowl and toss to coat.
3. Place the coated spears in a single layer in the air fryer basket or on the rack and roast at 400F for 5 minutes, or until the tips start to brown and the insides are cooked but not mushy. Serve warm.

Nutrition:
Calories: 46 Fat: 2g Carbohydrates: 5g Fiber: 3g Proteins: 3g

170. Twice-Baked Potatoes

Preparation time: 15 minutes Cooking time: 35 minutes Servings: 4

Ingredients:
- 2 medium russet potatoes, halved lengthwise
- ½ cup No-Cheese Sauce
- 2 scallions
- 1 tablespoon nutritional yeast

Directions:
1. Place each potato, cut-side down, on a scrap of parchment paper in the air fryer basket or on the rack. Roast at 400F for 30 minutes.

2. Carefully detach the potatoes from the air fryer. Set out the middle of each potato, leaving ¼ inch of flesh around the edges, and place the scooped parts in a medium bowl. Add the no-cheese sauce, scallions, and nutritional yeast to the bowl and mix until well combined.
3. Equally spoon the mixture into the potato skins and place them back in the air fryer. Grill at 400F for 3 to 4 minutes, or until the tops get crispy. Serve warm.

Nutrition:
Calories: 178 Fat: 21g Carbohydrates: 37g Fiber: 3g Proteins: 7g

171. Baba Ghanoush

Preparation time: 10 minutes   Cooking time: 30 minutes   Servings: 2

Ingredients:
- 1 medium eggplant
- 2 tablespoons tahini
- 2 tablespoons freshly squeezed lemon juice
- 1 teaspoon granulated garlic
- ¼ teaspoon ground cumin
- Freshly chopped parsley, for garnish

Directions:
1. Place the whole eggplant in a pan in the air fryer. Roast at 400°F for 30 minutes, carefully turning the eggplant over halfway through cooking.
2. Let the eggplant cool for 5 to 10 minutes. Then set out the flesh and set it in a medium bowl. Drain as much water from the eggplant flesh as possible.
3. Add the tahini, lemon juice, granulated garlic, and cumin to the bowl. Mix until well combined. Garnish with the parsley.

Nutrition:
Calories: 169 Fat: 9g Carbohydrates: 22g Fiber: 10g Proteins: 6g

172. Citrus-Roasted Brussels sprouts

Preparation time: 10 minutes   Cooking time: 10 minutes   Servings: 4

Ingredients:
- ¼ cup freshly squeezed orange juice
- 1 teaspoon pure maple syrup
- 1 tablespoon balsamic vinegar
- 1 pound Brussels sprouts, trimmed and quartered

Directions:
1. In a large bowl, set together the orange juice, maple syrup, and balsamic vinegar. Add the Brussels sprouts to the bowl and toss until well coated.
2. Place the Brussels sprouts, cut-side up, in a single layer in the air fryer basket or on the rack. Roast at 400F until they start to crisp up. Be careful not to burn them!

Nutrition:
Calories: 64 Fat: 0g Carbohydrates: 14g Fiber: 4g Proteins: 4g

173. Berry and Yogurt Smoothie

Preparation time: 5 minutes   Cooking time: 0 minutes.   Servings: 2

Ingredients:
- 2 small bananas
- 3 cups frozen mixed berries
- 1(½) cup cashew yogurt
- ½ teaspoon vanilla extract, unsweetened
- ½ cup almond milk, unsweetened

Directions:
1. Place all the ingredients in the order to a food processor or blender and then pulse for 2 to 3 minutes at high speed until smooth.
2. Pour the smoothie into two glasses and then serve.

Nutrition:
Calories: 326 Fat: 6.5g Carbohydrates: 65.6g Proteins: 8g Fiber: 8.4g

174. Basil Lime Green Tea

Preparation time: 5 minutes   Cooking time: 4 minutes   Servings: 8

Ingredients:
- 8 cups of filtered water
- 10 bags of green tea
- ¼ tsp. of maple syrup
- A pinch of baking soda
- Lime slices to taste
- Lemon slices to taste
- Basil leaves to taste

Directions:
1. Add water, maple syrup, and baking soda to the pot and mix. Add the tea bags and cover. Cook on High for 4 minutes. Open and serve with lime slices, lemon slices, and basil leaves.

Nutrition:
Calories: 32 Carbohydrates: 8g Fat: 0g Proteins: 0g

175. Pineapple and Spinach Juice

Preparation time: 5 minutes Cooking time: 0 minutes Servings: 2

Ingredients:
- 2 medium red apples, cored, peeled, chopped
- 3 cups spinach
- ½ of a medium pineapple, peeled
- 2 lemons, peeled

Directions:
1. Process all the ingredients in the order in a juicer or blender and then strain it into two glasses.
2. Serve straight away.

Nutrition:
Calories: 131 Fat: 0.5g Carbohydrates: 34.5g Proteins: 1.7g Fiber: 5g

176. Strawberry and Chocolate Milkshake

Preparation time: 5 minutes Cooking time: 0 minutes Servings: 2

Ingredients:
- 2 cups frozen strawberries
- 3 tablespoons cocoa powder
- 1 scoop protein powder
- 2 tablespoons maple syrup
- 1 teaspoon vanilla extract, unsweetened
- 2 cups almond milk, unsweetened

Directions:
1. Place all the ingredients in the order to a food processor or blender and then pulse for 2 to 3 minutes at high speed until smooth.
2. Pour the smoothie into two glasses and then serve.

Nutrition:
Calories: 199 Fat: 4.1g Carbohydrates: 40.5g Proteins: 3.7g Fiber: 5.5g

177. Fruit Infused Water

Preparation time: 5 minutes Cooking time: 0 minutes Servings: 2

Ingredients:
- 3 strawberries, sliced
- 5 mint leaves
- ½ of orange, sliced
- 2 cups of water

Directions:
1. Divide fruits and mint between two glasses, pour in water, stir until just mixed, and refrigerate for 2 hours.
2. Serve straight away.

Nutrition:
Calories: 5.4 Fat: 0.1g Carbohydrates: 1.3g Proteins: 0.1g Fiber: 0.4g

178. Lebanese Potato Salad

Preparation time: 5 minutes Cooking time: 10 minutes Servings: 4

Ingredients:
- 1-pound Russet potatoes
- 1(½) tablespoon extra-virgin olive oil
- 2 scallions, thinly sliced
- Freshly ground pepper to taste
- 2 tablespoons lemon juice
- ¼ tsp. salt or to taste

- 2 tablespoons fresh mint leaves, chopped

Directions:
1. Set a saucepan half-filled with water over medium heat. Add salt and potatoes and cook for 10 minutes until tender. Drain the potatoes and set them in a bowl of cold water. When cool enough to handle, peel and cube the potatoes. Place in a bowl.
2. To make the dressing: Add oil, lemon juice, salt, and pepper in a bowl and whisk well. Drizzle dressing over the potatoes. Toss well.
3. Add scallions and mint and toss well.
4. Divide into 4 plates and serve.

Nutrition:
Calories: 129 Fat: 0.9g Carbohydrates: 8.8g

179. Kale and Cauliflower Salad

Preparation time: 10 minutes Cooking time: 0 minutes Servings: 2

Ingredients:
- ½ cup lemon juice
- 1 tablespoon olive oil
- 1 teaspoon maple syrup
- ⅛ teaspoon salt
- ¼ teaspoon ground black pepper
- 1 bunch kale, cut into bite-size pieces
- ½ cup roasted cauliflower
- ½ cup dried cranberries

Directions:
1. Whisk lemon juice, olive oil, maple syrup, salt, and black pepper in a large bowl. Add kale, cauliflower, and cranberries; toss to combine.

Nutrition:
Calories: 76 Fat: 5 g Carbohydrates: 5.9 g

180. Creamy Lentil Dip

Preparation time: 10 minutes **Cooking time:** 15 minutes Servings: 3

Ingredients:
- 2½ cups water, divided
- 1 cup dried green or brown lentils, washed
- ⅓ cup tahini
- 1 garlic clove
- ½ teaspoon salt (optional)

Directions:
1. Stir together 2 cups of water and dried lentils in a medium pot and bring to a boil over high heat.
2. When it starts to heat, set the heat to low, secure, and let simmer until the lentils are soft, stirring occasionally for about 15 minutes. Drain any excess liquid.
3. Transfer the lentils to a food processor, along with the remaining ½ cup of water, tahini, garlic, and salt (if desired), and pulse until smooth and creamy.
4. Serve immediately.

Nutrition:
Calories: 101 Fat: 4.2g Carbohydrates: 10.8g Proteins: 5.0g Fiber: 6.0g

181. Easy Cucumber Dip

Preparation time: 5 minutes Cooking time: 0 minutes Servings: 11

Ingredients:
- 1 cucumber, peeled, cut in half lengthwise, deseeded and coarsely chopped
- 3 to 4 cloves garlic, crushed
- 1 cup plain soy yogurt
- ¼ teaspoon white pepper

Directions:
1. In a blender, blend the cucumber until finely chopped. Remove from the blend and place in a very fine strainer. Press out as much water as possible. Return to the blender.
2. Attach the remaining ingredients and process until smooth.
3. Refrigerate for several hours before serving.

Nutrition:
Calories: 48 Fat: 1.0g Carbohydrates: 6.2g Proteins: 3.6g Fiber: 0.4g

182. Ranch Cauliflower Dip

Preparation time: 15 minutes Cooking time: 0 minutes Servings: 8

Ingredients:
- 2 cups frozen cauliflower, thawed
- ½ cup unsweetened almond milk
- 2 tablespoons apple cider vinegar
- 2 tablespoons extra-virgin olive oil (Optional)
- 1 garlic clove, peeled
- 2 teaspoons finely chopped fresh parsley
- 2 teaspoons finely chopped scallions, both white and green parts
- 1 teaspoon finely chopped fresh dill
- ½ teaspoon onion powder
- ½ teaspoon Dijon mustard
- ½ teaspoon salt (optional)
- ¼ teaspoon freshly ground black pepper

Directions:
1. Press all the ingredients in a blender until smooth and combined.
2. Serve immediately or store in a sealed container in the refrigerator for up to 3 days.

Nutrition:
Calories: 51 Fat: 4.2g Carbohydrates: 2.1g Proteins: 1.2g Fiber: 1.1g

183. Sweet and Tangy Ketchup

Preparation time: 5 minutes **Cooking time:** 10 minutes Servings: 21

Ingredients:
- 1 cup water
- ¼ cup maple syrup
- 1 cup tomato paste
- 3 tablespoons apple cider vinegar
- 1 teaspoon onion powder
- 1 teaspoon garlic powder

Directions:
1. Attach the water to a medium saucepan and bring to a rolling boil over high heat.
2. Reduce the heat to low, set in the maple syrup, tomato paste, vinegar, onion powder, and garlic powder. Cover and bring to a gentle simmer for about 10 minutes, stirring frequently, or until the sauce begins to thicken and bubble.
3. Let the sauce rest for 30 minutes until cooled completely. Transfer to an airtight container and refrigerate for up to 1 month.

Nutrition:
Calories: 46 Fat: 5.2g Carbohydrates: 1.0g Proteins: 1.1g Fiber: 1.0g

184. Cilantro Coconut Pesto

Preparation time: 5 minutes Cooking time: 0 minutes Servings: 2

Ingredients:
- 1 (13.5-ounce / 383-g) can unsweetened coconut milk
- 2 jalapeños, seeds and ribs removed
- 1 bunch cilantro leaves only
- 1 tablespoon white miso
- 1-inch (2.5 cm) piece ginger, peeled and minced
- Water, as needed

Directions:
1. Set all the ingredients in a blender until creamy and smooth.
2. Thin with a little extra water as needed to reach your preferred consistency.
3. Set in an airtight bag in the fridge for up to 2 days or in the freezer for up to 6 months.

Nutrition:
Calories: 141 Fat: 13.7g Carbohydrates: 2.8g Proteins: 1.6g Fiber: 0.3g

185. Raw Cashew Pesto

Preparation time: 5 minutes Cooking time: 0 minutes Servings: 1

Ingredients:
- ⅓ red onion, about 2 ounces (57 g)
- Juice of 1 lemon
- 2 garlic cloves
- 4 cups packed basil leaves
- 1 cup wheatgrass
- ¼ cup raw cashews soak in boiling water for 5 minutes and drained
- ¼ cup water

- 1 tablespoon olive oil (optional)
- ¼ teaspoon salt (optional)

Directions:
1. Bring all the ingredients in a food processor and merge for 2 to 3 minutes, or until fully combined.
2. Serve immediately.

Nutrition:
Calories: 98 Fat: 7.3g Carbohydrates: 6.1g Proteins: 3.2g Fiber: 1.1g

186. Plantain Chips

Preparation time: 10 minutes **Cooking time:** 14 minutes Servings: 4

Ingredients:
- ¼ Teaspoon Cumin
- ½ Teaspoon Smoked Paprika
- 1 Green Plantain, Sliced

Directions:
1. Start by setting your grill to medium heat and then get out an aluminum sheet. Grease using cooking spray, and then spread out the plantain slices. Drizzle with paprika and cumin. Place this sheet on the grill.
2. Cover your grill and cook for seven minutes. Flip the plantain slices using a tong, and then cover again.
3. Cook for an additional seven minutes before serving the dish warm.

Nutrition:
Calories: 178 Fat: 21g Carbohydrates: 37g Fiber: 3g Proteins: 7g

187. Stuffed Portobello

Preparation time: 10 minutes **Cooking time:** 1 hour 20 minutes Servings: 6

Ingredients:
- ½ Cup Mint, Fresh
- ½ Cup Basil, Fresh
- 1 Cup Wild Rice
- ½ Cup Parsley, Fresh
- 1 Tablespoon Olive Oil
- 1 Tablespoon Nutritional Yeast
- 1 Lemon, Zested
- ½ Lemon, Juiced
- 1 tsp. maple syrup
- ¾ Cup Pecans
- 6 Portobello Mushrooms, Large
- Coconut Oil to Grease
- Sea Salt and Black Pepper to Taste

Directions:
1. Get a saucepan and place three cups of water in with your wild rice. Season with sea salt, and then place the lid on.
2. Cook your rice using a simmer for fifty minutes.
3. Drain the rice, and then spread your pecans on a baking sheet. Turn the oven to 375, and then roast for eight minutes. Shake once during this time.
4. Chop your pecans, and then set the chopped pecans to the side.
5. Blend your basil, olive oil, parsley, mint, lemon juice, zest, nutritional yeast, salt, and maple syrup in a blender.
6. Clean your mushrooms before brushing them down with coconut oil. Drizzle your mushrooms with salt and pepper, and then heat the grill to medium-high heat. Grill your mushrooms for six minutes per side, and then stuff each mushroom with pesto, wild rice, and your pecans. Garnish with lemon zest before serving.

Nutrition:
Calories: 199 Fat: 4.1g Carbohydrates: 40.5g Proteins: 3.7g Fiber: 5.5g

188. Easy Collard Greens

Preparation time: 10 minutes **Cooking time:** 25 minutes Servings: 4

Ingredients:
- Black Pepper to Taste
- ½ Teaspoon Onion Powder
- ½ Teaspoon Garlic Powder
- 1 Cup Vegetable Broth

- 1 ½ lb. Collard Greens

Directions:
1. Remove the hard stems and chop your leaves roughly. Get out a saucepan and mix your garlic powder, onion powder, pepper, and vegetable broth. Bring the mix to a boil using medium-high heat. Add in the greens and lower the heat to a simmer.
2. Cover the dish and cook for twenty minutes. Stir every five to six minutes. Serve warm.

Nutrition:
Calories: 371 Fat: 42.4g Carbohydrates: 42g Proteins: 5.5g Fiber: 2

189. Sesame Fries

Preparation time: 10 minutes **Cooking time:** 35 minutes Servings: 4

Ingredients:
- 1 lb. Gold Potatoes, Unpeeled and Sliced into Wedges
- 2 Tablespoons Sesame Seeds
- 1 Tablespoon Avocado Oil
- 1 Tablespoon Potato Starch
- 1 Tablespoon Nutritional Yeast
- Sea Salt and Black Pepper to Taste

Directions:
1. Heat your oven to 425, and then get out a baking tray. Line with parchment paper and put your potatoes onto the tray. Toss with remaining ingredients.
2. Bake for twenty-five minutes, tossing halfway through.

Nutrition:
Calories: 199 Fat: 4.1g Carbohydrates: 40.5g Proteins: 3.7g Fiber: 5.5g

190. French Potato Salad

Preparation time: 10 minutes **Cooking time:** 25 minutes Servings: 14

Ingredients:
Dressing:
- ¼ Cup Dill, Fresh and Chopped
- 3 Tablespoons Olive Oil
- 1 Tablespoon Apple Cider Vinegar
- 3 Tablespoons Red Wine Vinegar
- Sea Salt and Black Pepper to Taste
- 3 Cloves Garlic, Minced
- 2 ½ Tablespoons Spicy Brown Mustard
- Potatoes and Vegetables:
- 2 lb. Baby Yellow potatoes
- Sea Salt and Black Pepper to Taste
- 1 Tablespoon Apple Cider Vinegar
- 1 Cup Green Onion, Diced
- ¼ Cup Parsley, Fresh and Chopped

Directions:
1. Wash your potatoes before chopping them into ¼ inch slices. Put the slices in a pan, preferably a saucepan, and then add the water. Add a pinch of salt.
2. Boil for fifteen minutes. Your potatoes should be soft. Drain and rinse using cold water.
3. Add the potatoes to a serving bowl, seasoning with apple cider vinegar, and then a dash of salt and pepper.
4. Set all remaining ingredients together in a separate bowl. Mix well before serving.

Nutrition:
Calories: 679 Proteins: 25g Carbohydrates: 11g Fat: 62g

191. Vanilla Milk Steamer

Preparation time: 5 minutes Cooking time: 5 minutes Servings: 1

Ingredients:
- 1 cup unsweetened almond milk
- 2 teaspoons pure maple syrup (optional)
- ½ teaspoon pure vanilla extract
- Pinch ground cinnamon

Directions:
1. Warmth the almond milk in a small saucepan over medium heat for 5 minutes until steaming, stirring constantly (don't allow it to boil).

2. Carefully spill the hot milk into your blender and mix in the maple syrup (if desired) and vanilla. Blend on low speed, then set the speed to high and blend until well combined and frothy.
3. Serve sprinkled with the cinnamon.

Nutrition:
Calories: 184 Fat: 7.9g Carbohydrates: 20.7g Proteins: 7.6g Fiber: 0g

192. Cannellini Pesto Spaghetti

Preparation time: 5 minutes   **Cooking time:** 10 minutes   Servings: 4

Ingredients:
- 12 ounces (340 g) whole-grain spaghetti, cooked, drained, and kept warm,
- ½ cup cooking liquid reserved
- 1 cup pesto
- 2 cups cooked cannellini beans, drained and washed

Directions:
1. Put the cooked spaghetti in a large bowl and add the pesto.
2. Add the reserved cooking liquid and beans and toss well to serve.

Nutrition:
Calories: 549 Fat: 34.9g Carbohydrates: 45.2g Proteins: 18.3g Fiber: 10.1g

193. Cold Orange Soba Noodles

Preparation time: 10 minutes   Cooking time: 8 minutes   Servings: 4

Ingredients:
- 3 tablespoons mellow white miso
- Zest of 1 orange and of 2 oranges
- 3 tablespoons grated ginger
- ½ teaspoon crushed red pepper flakes
- 1 pound (454 g) soba noodles, cooked, drained, and rinsed until cool
- ¼ cup chopped cilantro
- 4 green onions, white and green parts

Directions:
1. Put the miso, orange zest and juice, ginger, and crushed red pepper flakes in a large bowl and whisk well to combine.
2. Add water as needed to make the sauce pourable. Add the cooked noodles and toss to coat well.
3. Set garnished with the cilantro and green onions.

Nutrition:
Calories: 166 Fat: 1.1g Carbohydrates: 34.2g Proteins: 7.9g Fiber: 1.3g

194. Indonesia Green Noodle Salad

Preparation time: 10 minutes   Cooking time: 8 minutes   Servings: 4

Ingredients:
- 12 ounces (340 g) brown rice noodles, cooked, drained, and rinsed until cool
- 1 cup snow peas, trimmed and sliced in half on the diagonal
- 2 medium cucumbers, peeled, halved, deseeded, and sliced thinly
- 2 heads baby bok choy, trimmed and thinly sliced
- 4 green onions, green and white parts, trimmed and thinly sliced
- 3 tablespoons sambal oelek
- ½ cup chopped cilantro
- 2 tablespoons soy sauce
- ¼ cup fresh lime juice
- ¼ cup finely chopped mint

Directions:
1. Merge all the ingredients in a large bowl and toss to coat well.
2. Serve immediately.

Nutrition:
Calories: 288 Fat: 1.1g Carbohydrates: 64.6g Proteins: 12.1g Fiber: 18.7g

195. Fruity Rice Pudding

Preparation time: 10 minutes   **Cooking time:** 30 minutes   Servings: 4

Ingredients:

- 1 cup crushed pineapple with juice, drained
- 2 cups cooked brown rice
- 2 tablespoons raisins
- 1 banana, peeled and chopped
- ½ cup fresh orange juice
- 1 tablespoon vanilla extract
- ¾ cup water

Directions:
1. Warmth the oven to 350F.
2. Merge the pineapple, rice, and raisins in a bowl.
3. Set the remaining ingredients in a food processor and process until smooth. Fold the mixture into the rice mixture.
4. Pour into a casserole dish. Secure and bake in the preheated oven for 30 minutes.
5. Serve immediately.

Nutrition:
Calories: 199 Fat: 4.1g Carbohydrates: 40.5g Proteins: 3.7g Fiber: 5.5g

196. Oat Cookies

Preparation time: 30 minutes **Cooking time:** 15 minutes Servings: 40

Ingredients:
- 2 cups rolled oats
- 1 cup whole-wheat flour
- ¼ cup soy flour
- ¼ cup wheat bran
- ¼ cup oat bran
- 1 teaspoon baking soda
- 1 tablespoon baking powder
- 2 teaspoons ground cinnamon
- ½ cup unsweetened pineapple juice
- ½ cup fresh apple juice
- ½ cup raisins
- ½ cup chopped dates
- 2 teaspoons vanilla extract
- ¾ cup maple syrup (optional)

Directions:
1. Warmth the oven to 350F.
2. Merge the dry ingredients in a large bowl. Fold in the remaining ingredients. Stir to mix well.
3. Drop 1 tablespoon of the mixture on a baking sheet to make a cookie. Repeat with remaining mixture.
4. Bake in the warm oven for 15 to 20 minutes.
5. Serve immediately.

Nutrition:
Calories: 34 Carbohydrates: 4g Proteins: 45g Fat: 3g

197. Sweet Potato Tater Tots

Preparation time: 30 minutes **Cooking time:** 15 minutes Servings: 4

Ingredients:
- 1 ½ pounds sweet potatoes, grated
- 2 chia eggs
- ½ cup plain flour
- ½ cup breadcrumbs
- 3 tablespoons hummus
- Sea salt and black pepper, to taste
- 1 tablespoon olive oil
- ½ cup salsa sauce

Directions:
1. Start by preheating your oven to 395 F. Line a baking pan with parchment paper or Silpat mat.
2. Thoroughly merge all the ingredients, except for the salsa, until everything is well incorporated.
3. Roll the batter into equal balls and place them in your refrigerator for about 1 hour.
4. Bake these balls for approximately 25 minutes, turning them over halfway through the cooking time. Bon appétit!

Nutrition:
Calories: 98 Fat: 7.3g Carbohydrates: 6.1g Proteins: 3.2g Fiber: 1.1g

198. Roasted Pepper and Tomato Dip

Preparation time: 30 minutes **Cooking time:** 35 minutes Servings: 10

Ingredients:

- 4 red bell peppers
- 4 tomatoes
- 4 tablespoons olive oil
- 1 red onion, chopped
- 4 garlic cloves
- 4 ounces canned garbanzo beans, drained
- Sea salt and ground black pepper

Directions:
1. Warmth your oven to 400 F.
2. Place the peppers and tomatoes on a parchment-lined baking pan. Bake for about 30 minutes; peel the peppers and transfer them to your food processor along with the roasted tomatoes.
3. Meanwhile, warmth 2 tablespoons of the olive oil in a frying pan over medium-high heat. Sauté the onion and garlic for about 5 minutes or until they've softened.
4. Add the sautéed vegetables to your food processor. Add in the garbanzo beans, salt, pepper and the remaining olive oil, process until creamy and smooth.
5. Bon appétit!

Nutrition:
Calories: 371 Fat: 42.4g Carbohydrates: 42g Proteins: 5.5g Fiber: 2g

199. Seeds Crackers

Preparation time: 30 minutes   **Cooking time:** 35 minutes   Servings: 6

Ingredients:
- 3 tablespoons water
- 1 tablespoon chia seeds
- 3 tablespoons sunflower seeds
- 1 tablespoon quinoa flour
- 1 teaspoon ground turmeric
- Pinch of ground cinnamon
- Salt, to taste

Directions:
1. Preheat your oven to 345F Line a baking sheet with parchment paper.
2. In a bowl, add the water and chia seeds and set aside for about 15 minutes.
3. Then attach the remaining ingredients and mix well.
4. Spread the mixture onto the prepared baking sheet evenly.
5. Bake for about 20 minutes.
6. Detach from the oven and place onto a wire rack to cool completely before serving.
7. Break into pieces and serve.

Nutrition:
Calories: 34 Carbohydrates: 4g Proteins: 45g Fat: 3g

200. Spicy Almonds

Preparation time: 30 minutes   **Cooking time:** 10 minutes   Servings: 4

Ingredients:
- 2 cups whole almonds
- 1 tablespoon chili powder
- ½ teaspoon ground cinnamon
- ½ teaspoon ground cumin
- ½ teaspoon ground coriander
- Salt and black pepper, to taste
- 1 tablespoon olive oil

Directions:
1. Preheat your oven to 375F.
2. Line a suitable baking pan with parchment paper.
3. Toss almonds with all the spices and oil.
4. Spread the almond mixture into the prepared baking dish in a single layer.
5. Roast for about 10 minutes, flipping twice.
6. Detach from the oven and let it cool completely before serving.

Nutrition:
Calories: 456 Fat: 33g Carbohydrates: 37g Proteins: 8.3g Fiber: 5g

Dessert

201. Berries Pie

Preparation time: 10 minutes **Cooking time:** 24 minutes Servings: 12

Ingredients:
- 2 cups coconut flour
- 1 cup coconut butter, soft
- 1 cup pecans, chopped
- 1 and ¼ cup coconut sugar
- 4 cups rhubarb, chopped
- 1 cup strawberries, sliced
- 8 ounces coconut cream

Directions:
1. In a bowl, merge the flour with the butter, pecans and ¼ cup of sugar and mix well.
2. Transfer this to a cake pan, press firmly into the pan, place in the oven and bake at 350F for 20 minutes.
3. In a pan combine the strawberries with the remaining ingredients, mix well and cook over medium heat for 4 minutes.
4. Spread it on the crust of the cake and keep it in the fridge for a few hours before slicing and serving.

Nutrition:
Calories: 332 Fat: 5g Fiber: 5g Carbohydrates: 15g Proteins: 6.3g

202. Vanilla and Apple Brownies

Preparation time: 10 minutes **Cooking time:** 20 minutes Servings: 12

Ingredients:
- 1 and ½ cups apples, cored and cubed
- 2 tablespoons stevia
- ½ cup quick oats
- 2 tablespoons cocoa powder
- ⅓ cup coconut cream
- ¼ cup coconut oil, melted
- ½ teaspoon baking powder
- 2 teaspoons vanilla extract
- Cooking spray

Directions:
1. In your food processor, combine the apples with the stevia and the other ingredients except for the cooking spray and blend well.
2. Grease a square pan with cooking spray, add the apples mix, spread, introduce in the oven, and bake at 350F for 20 minutes, leave aside to cool down, slice, and serve.

Nutrition:
Calories: 200 Fat: 3g Fiber: 3g Carbohydrates: 14g Proteins: 4g

203. Banana Cake

Preparation time: 10 minutes   **Cooking time:** 25 minutes   Servings: 8

Ingredients:
- 2 cups almond flour
- ¼ cup cocoa powder
- 1 banana, peeled and mashed
- ½ teaspoon baking soda
- ½ cup coconut sugar
- ¾ cup almond milk
- ¼ cup coconut oil, melted
- 2 tablespoons flaxseed mixed with 3 tablespoons water
- 1 teaspoon vanilla extract
- 1 tablespoon lemon juice
- Cooking spray

Directions:
1. In a bowl, merge the flour with the cocoa powder, banana, and the other ingredients except for the cooking spray and stir well.
2. Grease a cake pan with cooking spray, pour the cake mix, spread, bake in the oven at 350F for 25 minutes, cool down, slice, and serve.

Nutrition:
Calories: 245 Fat: 5.6g Fiber: 4g Carbohydrates: 17g Proteins: 4g

204. Coconut Mousse

Preparation time: 10 minutes   Cooking time: 0 minutes   Servings: 12

Ingredients:
- 2 and ¾ cup almond milk
- 2 tablespoons cocoa powder
- 1 teaspoon coconut extract
- 1 teaspoon vanilla extract
- 4 teaspoons stevia
- 1 cup coconut, toasted

Directions:
1. In a bowl, merge the almond milk with cocoa powder and the other ingredients, whisk well, divide into small cups and serve cold.

Nutrition:
Calories: 352 Fat: 5.4g Fiber: 5.4g Carbohydrates: 11g Proteins: 3g

205. Mango Coconut Pudding

Preparation time: 10 minutes   **Cooking time:** 50 minutes   Servings: 4

Ingredients:
- 1 cup coconut, shredded
- 1 cup coconut cream
- 1 mango, peeled and chopped
- 1 cup coconut milk
- 2 tablespoons coconut sugar
- 1 teaspoon vanilla extract
- ½ teaspoon cinnamon powder

Directions:
1. In a pan, mix the coconut with the cream and the other ingredients, stir, simmer for 50 minutes over medium heat, divide into bowls and serve cold.

Nutrition:
Calories: 251 Fat: 3.6g Fiber: 4g Carbohydrates: 16g Proteins: 7.1g

206. Rhubarb and Berries Pie

Preparation time: 10 minutes   **Cooking time:** 25 minutes   Servings: 12

Ingredients:
- 2 cups coconut flour
- 1 cup coconut butter, soft

- 1 cup pecans, chopped
- 1 and ¼ cup coconut sugar
- 4 cups rhubarb, chopped
- 1 cup strawberries, sliced
- 8 ounces coconut cream

Directions:
1. In a bowl, merge the flour with the butter, pecans, and ¼ cup sugar and stir well.
2. Transfer this to a pie pan, press well into the pan, introduce it in the oven and bake at 350F for 20 minutes.
3. In a pan, combine the strawberries with the remaining ingredients, stir well and cook over medium heat for 4 minutes.
4. Spread this over the pie crust and keep it in the fridge for a few hours before slicing and serving.

Nutrition:
Calories: 332 Fat: 6g Fiber: 5g Carbohydrates: 15g Proteins: 6.3g

207. Banana Salad

Preparation time: 10 minutes Cooking time: 0 minutes Servings: 2

Ingredients:
- ¼ cantaloupe, cubed
- 3 bananas, cut into chunks
- 1 apple, cored and cut into chunks
- 1 tablespoon stevia
- 1 teaspoon vanilla extract
- Juice of 1 lime

Directions:
1. In a bowl, merge the cantaloupe with the bananas and the other ingredients, toss and serve.

Nutrition:
Calories: 126 Fat: 3.3g Fiber: 1g Carbohydrates: 1.2g Proteins: 2g

208. Lemon Berries

Preparation time: 10 minutes **Cooking time:** 10 minutes Servings: 6

Ingredients:
- 2 teaspoons lemon juice
- 2 teaspoons lemon zest, grated
- Juice of 1 apple
- 1 teaspoon vanilla extract
- 1 pound blackberries
- 1 pound strawberries
- 4 tablespoons stevia

Directions:
1. In a pan, mix the berries with the stevia and the other ingredients, stir and cook over medium heat for 10 minutes.
2. Divide into cups and serve cold.

Nutrition:
Calories: 170 Fat: 3.4g Fiber: 3g Carbohydrates: 4g Proteins: 4g

209. Peach Stew

Preparation time: 10 minutes **Cooking time:** 10 minutes Servings: 6

Ingredients:
- 1 pound peaches, peeled and chopped
- 2 tablespoons water
- 2 tablespoons stevia
- 2 tablespoons lemon juice
- ¼ teaspoon almond extract

Directions:
1. In a pot, combine the peaches with the water and the other ingredients, toss well, cook over medium heat for 10 minutes, divide into bowls and serve.

Nutrition:
Calories: 160 Fat: 3.8g Fiber: 2g Carbohydrates: 6g Proteins: 6g

210. Apple Stew

Preparation time: 10 minutes **Cooking time:** 15 minutes Servings: 6

Ingredients:
- 6 apples, cored and roughly chopped
- 4 tablespoons stevia

- 2 teaspoons vanilla extract
- 2 teaspoons lime juice
- 2 teaspoons cinnamon powder

Directions:
1. In a small pan, combine the apples with the stevia and the other ingredients, heat up and cook for about 10-15 minutes, divide between small dessert plates and serve.

Nutrition:
Calories: 210 Fat: 7.3g Fiber: 3g Carbohydrates: 8g Proteins: 5g

211. Minty Apricots

Preparation time: 10 minutes	**Cooking time:** 10 minutes	Servings: 4

Ingredients:
- ⅓ cup water
- 2 pounds apricots, chopped
- 3 tablespoons stevia
- 1 tablespoon mint, chopped

Directions:
1. In a pot, mix the apricots with the stevia and the other ingredients, stir, cook for 10 minutes, divide into bowls and serve.

Nutrition:
Calories: 160 Fat: 5.1g Fiber: 4g Carbohydrates: 8g Proteins: 5.2g

212. Mango Mix

Preparation time: 10 minutes	**Cooking time:** 10 minutes	Servings: 8

Ingredients:
- 1 and ½ pounds mango, peeled and cubed
- 3 tablespoons stevia
- 1 cup orange juice
- ½ tablespoon lime juice
- 1 teaspoon vanilla extract

Directions:
1. In a small pot, combine the mango with the stevia, orange juice, and the other ingredients, toss, bring to a parboil over medium heat, cook for 10 minutes, divide into bowls and serve.

Nutrition:
Calories: 160 Fat: 5.4g Fiber: 4g Carbohydrates: 8g Proteins: 3.4g

213. Blueberry Stew

Preparation time: 10 minutes	Cooking time: 10 minutes	Servings: 4

Ingredients:
- 2 tablespoons lemon juice
- 3 tablespoons stevia
- 12 ounces blueberries
- 1 cup orange juice
- 1 teaspoon vanilla extract

Directions:
1. In a pot, mix the blueberries with the stevia and the other ingredients, stir, cook over medium heat for 10 minutes, divide into small cups and serve cold.

Nutrition:
Calories: 201 Fat: 3g Fiber: 2g Carbohydrates: 6g Proteins: 3.8g

214. Lime Cream

Preparation time: 10 minutes	**Cooking time:** 15 minutes	Servings: 4

Ingredients:
- 3 cups coconut milk
- Juice of 2 limes
- Lemon zest of 2 limes, grated
- 3 tablespoons stevia
- 3 tablespoons coconut oil
- 2 tablespoons gelatin
- 1 cup water

Directions:
1. In your blender, mix coconut milk with lime juice and the other ingredients except for the water and blend well.
2. Divide this into small jars and seal them.

3. Put the jars in a pan, add the water, introduce in the oven and cook at 380 degrees F for 15 minutes.
4. Serve the cream cold.

Nutrition:
Calories: 161 Fat: 3.4g Fiber: 5g Carbohydrates: 6g Proteins: 4g

215. Vanilla Peach Mix

Preparation time: 10 minutes **Cooking time:** 10 minutes Servings: 4

Ingredients:
- 4 cups water
- 3 peaches, chopped
- 2 cups rolled oats
- 1 teaspoon vanilla extract
- 2 tablespoons flax meal

Directions:
1. In a pan, combine the peaches with the water and the other ingredients, stir, bring to a parboil over medium heat, cook for 10 minutes, divide into bowls and serve.

Nutrition:
Calories: 161 Fat: 3g Fiber: 3g Carbohydrates: 7g Proteins: 5g

216. Pear Stew

Preparation time: 10 minutes **Cooking time:** 10 minutes Servings: 4

Ingredients:
- 3 pears, cored and chopped
- 2 tablespoons stevia
- ¼ cup coconut, shredded
- ½ teaspoon cinnamon powder
- 3 tablespoons coconut oil, melted
- ¼ cup pecans, chopped

Directions:
1. In a pan, combine pears with the stevia and the other ingredients, stir, cook for 8 minutes, divide into bowls and serve cold.

Nutrition:
Calories: 142 Fat: 4g Fiber: 4g Carbohydrates: 7.2g Proteins: 7g

217. Mango Shake

Preparation time: 5 minutes Cooking time: 0 minutes Servings: 2

Ingredients:
- 2 medium mangoes, peeled
- 2 teaspoons cocoa powder
- ½ big avocado, mashed
- ¾ cup almond milk
- 1 tablespoon stevia

Directions:
1. In a blender, mix the mangoes with the cocoa powder and the other ingredients, blend, divide into glasses and serve.

Nutrition:
Calories: 185 Fat: 3.4g Fiber: 4.2g Carbohydrates: 6g Proteins: 7g

218. Lime Bars

Preparation time: 30 minutes Cooking time: 0 minutes Servings: 4

Ingredients:
- 1 cup avocado oil
- 2 bananas, peeled and chopped
- A pinch of salt
- 3 tablespoons stevia
- ¼ cup lime juice
- A pinch of lime zest, grated
- Cooking spray
- 3 kiwis, peeled and chopped

Directions:
1. In a food processor, mix the oil with the bananas and the other ingredients except for the cooking spray pulse and spread it into a pan after you've greased it with the cooking spray.
2. Keep in the fridge for 30 minutes, slice, and serve bars.

Nutrition:
Calories: 187 Fat: 3g Fiber: 3g Carbohydrates: 4g Proteins: 4g

219. Blackberry Cobbler

Preparation time: 10 minutes   **Cooking time:** 30 minutes   Servings: 6

Ingredients:
- ¾ cup coconut sugar
- 6 cups blackberries
- ⅛ teaspoon baking soda
- 1 tablespoon lemon juice
- ½ cup almond flour
- A pinch of salt
- ½ cup water
- 3 and ½ tablespoon avocado oil
- Cooking spray

Directions:
1. Set a baking dish with some cooking spray and leave it aside.
2. In a bowl, mix blackberries with half of the coconut sugar, sprinkle some flour and add lemon juice, whisk and pour into the baking dish.
3. In another bowl, mix flour with remaining sugar, a pinch of salt, baking soda, ½ cup water, and the oil and stir well with your hands.
4. Spread over berries, bake at 375 degrees F for 30 minutes, cool down, and serve.

Nutrition:
Calories: 221 Fat: 7.3g Fiber: 3.3g Carbohydrates: 6g Proteins: 9g

220. Black Tea Cake

Preparation time: 10 minutes   **Cooking time:** 35 minutes   Servings: 12

Ingredients:
- 6 tablespoons black tea powder
- 2 cups almond milk
- ½ cup coconut butter
- 2 cups coconut sugar
- 2 tablespoons flaxseed mixed with 3 tablespoons water
- 2 teaspoons vanilla extract
- ½ cup olive oil
- 3 and ½ cups almond flour
- 1 teaspoon baking soda
- 3 teaspoons baking powder

Directions:
1. In a large bowl, mix the black tea powder with the almond milk, coconut butter, and the other ingredients and stir well.
2. Pour this into a lined cake pan, place in the oven at 350 degrees F and bake for 30 minutes. Leave cakes to cool down.
3. Slice and serve.

Nutrition:
Calories: 200 Fat: 6.5g Fiber: 4g Carbohydrates: 6.5g Proteins: 4.5g

221. Green Tea Avocado Pudding

Preparation time: 2 hours   Cooking time: 5 minutes   Servings: 6

Ingredients:
- 2 cups almond milk
- 2 tablespoons green tea powder
- 1 cup coconut cream
- 3 tablespoons stevia
- 1 avocado, peeled, pitted, and mashed
- 1 teaspoon gelatin powder

Directions:
1. In a pan, mix the almond milk with green tea powder and the other ingredients, stir, cook for 5 minutes, divide into cups and keep in the fridge for 2 hours before serving.

Nutrition:
Calories: 210 Fat: 4.4g Fiber: 3g Carbohydrates: 7g Proteins: 4g

222. Pineapple and Mango Oatmeal

Preparation time: 5 minutes   Cooking time: 0 minutes   Servings: 2

Ingredients:
- 2 cups unsweetened almond milk
- 2 cups rolled oats
- ½ cup pineapple chunks, thawed if frozen
- ½ cup diced mango, thawed if frozen

- 1 banana, sliced
- 1 tablespoon chia seeds
- 1 tablespoon maple syrup

Directions:
1. Stir together the almond milk, oats, pineapple, mango, banana, chia seeds, and maple syrup in a large bowl until you see no clumps.
2. Secure and refrigerate to chill for at least 4 hours, preferably overnight.
3. Serve chilled with your favorite toppings.

Nutrition:
Calories: 512 Fat: 22.1g Carbohydrates: 13.1g Proteins: 14.1g Fiber: 15.2g

223. Breakfast Quinoa

Preparation time: 5 minutes **Cooking time:** 10 minutes Servings: 2

Ingredients:
- 1 cup unsweetened almond milk
- 2 cups cooked quinoa
- 1 tablespoon defatted peanut powder
- 1 tablespoon cocoa powder
- 1 tablespoon maple syrup

Directions:
1. Add the almond milk to a saucepan over medium-high heat and bring to a boil.
2. Set the heat to low, and add the quinoa, peanut powder, cocoa powder, and maple syrup while whisking.
3. Allow to simmer for 6 minutes, stirring frequently, or until some liquid has evaporated.
4. Remove from the heat and serve warm.

Nutrition:
Calories: 340 Fat: 18.2g Carbohydrates: 3.1g Proteins: 14.2g Fiber: 7.1g

224. Strawberry Chia Jam

Preparation time: 10 minutes **Cooking time:** 20 minutes Servings: 2

Ingredients:
- 1 pound (454 g) fresh strawberries, hulled and halved
- ¼ cup maple syrup
- ¼ cup water
- 3 tbsp. freshly squeezed lemon juice (from 1 lemon)
- 3 tablespoons chia seeds
- 1 teaspoon vanilla extract

Directions:
1. Add the strawberries, maple syrup, water, and lemon juice to a medium saucepan over medium heat. Allow to parboil for about 15 minutes, stirring occasionally, or until the strawberries begin to soften and bubble. Mash the strawberries to your desired consistency.
2. Add the chia seeds and continue stirring over low heat for 5 minutes. The chia seeds will help the jam achieve a gelatinous texture.
3. Add the vanilla and stir until combined. Detach from the heat and let the jam cool to room temperature. Stir again.
4. Serve immediately.

Nutrition:
Calories: 132 Fat: 2.5g Carbohydrates: 25.7g Proteins: 1.9g Fiber: 2.5g

225. Sticky Rice Congee with Dates

Preparation time: 10 minutes **Cooking time:** 15 minutes Servings: 4

Ingredients:
- 2 cups water
- 4 cups cooked brown rice
- ½ cup chopped apricots
- ½ cup dates, pitted and chopped
- ¼ teaspoon ground cloves
- 1 large cinnamon stick
- Salt, to taste (optional)

Directions:
1. Add 2 cups of water to a large saucepan over medium heat and bring to a boil.

2. Add the brown rice, apricots, dates, cloves, and cinnamon stick, and stir well.
3. Set the heat to medium-low and parboil for 15 minutes, stirring occasionally, or until the mixture is thickened. Sprinkle the salt to season, if desired.
4. Let the congee cool for 5 minutes and remove the cinnamon stick, then serve.

Nutrition:
Calories: 313 Fat: 1.9g Carbohydrates: 68.8g Proteins: 6.0g Fiber: 6.2g

226. Easy Apple and Cinnamon Muesli

Preparation time: 10 minutes   Cooking time: 0 minutes   Servings: 2

Ingredients:
- 1 cup rolled oats
- ½ cup raisins
- ¾ cup unsweetened almond milk
- 2 tablespoons date molasses (optional)
- ¼ teaspoon ground cinnamon
- 1 Granny Smith apple, grated

Directions:
1. In a large bowl, merge the oats, raisins, almond milk, date molasses (if desired), and cinnamon. Stir until well combined and transfer the bowl to the fridge. Let the oats soak for at least 30 minutes.
2. Remove from the fridge and add the grated apple. Give it a good stir and serve immediately.

Nutrition:
Calories: 325 Fat: 4.2g Carbohydrates: 63.7g Proteins: 8.8g Fiber: 10.1g

227. Salted Caramel Oatmeal

Preparation time: 5 minutes   **Cooking time:** 15 minutes   Servings: 4

Ingredients:
- 4 cups water
- 16 Medjool dates, pitted and chopped
- Pinch salt (optional)
- 2 cups steel-cut oats
- Fresh berries, for topping (optional)
- Sliced almonds, for topping (optional)

Directions:
1. Put the water, dates, and salt (if desired) in a small saucepan over high heat and bring to a rapid boil.
2. Once it starts to boil. Add the oats and allow to simmer for 10 minutes, stirring frequently, or until the oats are cooked through.
3. Divide the oatmeal among four serving bowls. Serve topped with fresh berries and sliced almonds, if desired.

Nutrition:
Calories: 376 Fat: 2.1g Carbohydrates: 84.9g Proteins: 5.2g Fiber: 9.1g

228. Creamy Brown Rice Cereal with Raisins

Preparation time: 5 minutes   **Cooking time:** 10 minutes   Servings: 2

Ingredients:
- 2 cups water
- ½ cup uncooked brown rice
- ¼ cup raisins
- 1½ cups unsweetened almond milk (optional)
- ½ teaspoon cinnamon (optional)

Directions:
1. Add the water to a medium saucepan over medium-high heat and bring to a boil.
2. Meanwhile, pulverize the brown rice by using a high-speed blender or food processor. Grind until the rice resembles sand.
3. Once it starts to boil, gradually stir in the ground brown rice.
4. Add the raisins and set the heat to low. Secure and simmer for 5 to 8 minutes, stirring once or twice during cooking, or until the rice is tender.
5. Sprinkle with the almond milk and cinnamon, if desired.

Nutrition:
Calories: 131 Fat: 1.8g Carbohydrates: 26.5g Proteins: 2.4g Fiber: 1.3g

229. Cashew-Date Waffles

Preparation time: 20 minutes   **Cooking time:** 10 minutes   Servings: 2

Ingredients:
- 1 ounce (28 g) raw, unsalted cashews (about ¼ cup)
- 1 ounce (28 g) pitted dates, chopped
- 2 cups unsweetened coconut milk
- 1½ cups old-fashioned rolled oats
- ½ cup cornmeal
- 2 teaspoons baking powder
- ½ teaspoon cinnamon

Directions:
1. In a small bowl, add the cashews, dates, and coconut milk. Let the nuts and dates soak in the milk for at least 15 minutes.
2. Merge the rolled oats in a blender until it has reached a powdery consistency.
3. Place the oats in a medium bowl, along with the cornmeal, baking powder, and cinnamon. Stir well and set aside.
4. Preheat the waffle iron to medium-high heat.
5. Blend the cashews, dates, and coconut milk in a blender until completely mixed. Spill the mixture into the bowl of dry ingredients and whisk to combine. Let the batter sit for 1 minute.
6. Slowly pour ½ to ¾ cup of the batter into the preheated waffle iron and cook until golden brown. Repeat with the remaining batter.
7. Divide the waffles between two plates and serve warm.

Nutrition:
Calories: 849 Fat: 13.5g Carbohydrates: 66.4g Proteins: 16.8g Fiber: 10.1g

230. Maple Sunflower Seed Granola

Preparation time: 20 minutes Cooking time: 0 minutes Servings: 2

Ingredients:
- 1½ cups peanut butter
- ¼ cup maple syrup
- 1½ cups old-fashioned rolled oats
- ¾ cup raw sunflower seeds
- ¾ cup flaxseed meal

Directions:
1. Set the peanut butter and maple syrup in a microwave-safe bowl, and microwave on high, stirring well between each interval, until the mixture is completely mixed. Let it rest for a few minutes until slightly cooled.
2. Add the rolled oats, sunflower seeds, and flaxseed meal to the bowl, and whisk until well incorporated.
3. Set the mixture to a baking sheet lined with parchment paper and spread it out into an even layer.
4. Transfer the baking sheet in the freezer for at least 25 minutes until firm.
5. Remove from the freezer and break the granola into large chunks before serving.

Nutrition:
Calories: 764 Fat: 51.7g Carbohydrates: 47.8g Proteins: 27.0g Fiber: 16.0g

231. Vegan Dairy Free Breakfast Bowl

Preparation time: 20 minutes Cooking time: 0 minutes Servings: 2

Ingredients:
- ½ cup strawberries
- ½ cup blueberries
- ½ cup blackberries
- ½ cup raspberries
- 1 grapefruit, peeled and segmented
- 3 tbs. fresh orange juice (from 1 orange)
- 1 tablespoon pure maple syrup
- ¼ cup chopped fresh mint
- ¼ cup sliced almonds

Directions:
1. In a serving bowl, combine the berries and grapefruit.
2. In a bowl, stir together the orange juice and maple syrup.
3. Pour the syrup mixture over the fruit. Sprinkle it with the mint and almonds. Serve immediately

Nutrition:
Calories: 199 Fat: 4g Fiber: 3g Carbohydrates: 12g Proteins: 9g

232. Hot and Healthy Breakfast Bowl with Nuts

Preparation time: 5 minutes Cooking time: 0 minutes Servings: 1

Ingredients:
- ½ cup oats, or quinoa flakes
- 1 tablespoon ground flaxseed, or chia seeds, or hemp hearts
- 1 tablespoon maple syrup or coconut sugar (optional)
- ¼ teaspoon ground cinnamon (optional)
- 1 apple, chopped and 1 tablespoon walnuts
- 2 tablespoons dried cranberries and 1 tablespoon pumpkin seeds
- 1 pear, chopped and 1 tablespoon cashews
- 1 cup sliced grapes and 1 tablespoon sunflower seeds
- 1 banana, sliced, and 1 tablespoon peanut butter
- 2 tablespoons raisins and 1 tablespoon hazelnuts
- 1 cup berries and 1 tablespoon unsweetened coconut flakes

Directions:
1. Mix the oats, flax, maple syrup, and cinnamon (if using) together in a bowl or to-go container (a travel mug or short thermos works beautifully).
2. Pour enough cool water over the oats to submerge them and stir to combine. Leave to soak for a minimum of half an hour, or overnight.
3. Add your choice of toppings.
4. Boil about ½ cup water and pour over the oats. Let them soak for about 5 minutes before eating.

Nutrition:
Calories: 244 Fat: 16g Carbohydrates: 10g Fiber: 6g Proteins: 7g

233. Healthy Chocolate Oats Bites

Preparation time: 15 minutes **Cooking time:** 12 minutes Servings: 2

Ingredients:
- 1 tablespoon ground flaxseed
- 2 tbsp. almond butter or sunflower seed butter
- 2 tablespoons maple syrup
- 1 banana, mashed
- 1 teaspoon ground cinnamon
- ¼ teaspoon ground nutmeg (optional)
- Pinch sea salt
- ½ cup rolled oats
- ¼ cup raisins, or dark chocolate chips

Directions:
1. Preheat the oven to 350F. Set a large baking sheet with parchment paper. Merge the ground flax with just enough water to cover it in a small dish and leave it to sit.
2. In a large bowl, merge together the almond butter and maple syrup until creamy, then attach the banana. Add the flax-water mixture.
3. Sift the cinnamon, nutmeg, and salt into a separate bowl, and then stir into the wet mixture. Attach the oats and raisins, and fold in.
4. From 3 to 4 tbsp. batter into a ball and press lightly to flatten onto the baking sheet. Repeat, spacing the cookies 2 to 3 inches apart. Bake for 12 minutes until golden brown.
5. Set the cookies in an airtight bag in the fridge.

Nutrition:
Calories: 192 Fat: 16g Carbohydrates: 4g Fiber: 4g Proteins: 4g

234. Homemade Nutty Fruity Muffins

Preparation time: 15 minutes **Cooking time:** 30 minutes Servings: 6

Ingredients:
- 1 teaspoon coconut oil, for greasing muffin tins (optional)
- 2 tbsp. almond butter, or sunflower seed butter
- ¼ cup non-dairy milk
- 1 orange, peeled
- 1 carrot, coarsely chopped
- 2 tbsp. chopped dried apricots, or other dried fruit
- 3 tablespoons molasses

- 2 tablespoons ground flaxseed
- 1 teaspoon apple cider vinegar
- 1 teaspoon pure vanilla extract
- ½ teaspoon ground cinnamon
- ½ teaspoon ground ginger (optional)
- ¼ teaspoon ground nutmeg (optional)
- ¼ teaspoon allspice (optional)
- ¾ cup rolled oats, or whole-grain flour
- 1 teaspoon baking powder
- ½ teaspoon baking soda

Mix-Ins (Optional):
- ½ cup rolled oats
- 2 tbsp. raisins, or other chopped dried fruit
- 2 tablespoons sunflower seeds

Directions:
1. Preheat the oven to 350F. Prepare a 6-cup muffin tin by rubbing the insides of the cups with coconut oil or using silicone or paper muffin cups.
2. Purée the nut butter, milk, orange, carrot, apricots, molasses, flaxseed, vinegar, vanilla, cinnamon, ginger, nutmeg, and allspice in a food processor until somewhat smooth.
3. Grind the oats in a clean coffee grinder until they're the consistency of flour (or use whole-grain flour). In a bowl, mix the oats with the baking powder and baking soda.
4. Mix the wet ingredients into the dry ingredients until just combined. Fold in the mix-ins (if using).
5. Set about ¼ cup batter into each muffin cup and bake for 30 minutes.

Nutrition:
Calories: 287 Fat: 23g Carbohydrates: 11g Fiber: 6g Proteins: 8g

235. Vanilla Flavored Whole Grain Muffins

Preparation time: 15 minutes **Cooking time:** 20 minutes Servings: 12

Ingredients:
- 1 teaspoon coconut oil, for greasing muffin tins (optional)
- 2 tablespoons nut butter or seed butter
- 1½ cups unsweetened applesauce
- ⅓ cup coconut sugar
- ½ cup non-dairy milk
- 2 tablespoons ground flaxseed
- 1 teaspoon apple cider vinegar
- 1 teaspoon pure vanilla extract
- 2 cups whole-grain flour
- 1 teaspoon baking soda
- ½ teaspoon baking powder
- 1 teaspoon ground cinnamon
- Pinch sea salt
- ½ cup walnuts, chopped

Toppings (Optional):
- ¼ cup walnuts
- ¼ cup coconut sugar
- ½ teaspoon ground cinnamon

Directions:
1. Preheat the oven to 350F. Prepare two 6-cup muffin tins by rubbing the insides of the cups with coconut oil or using silicone or paper muffin cups.
2. In a large bowl, mix the nut butter, applesauce, coconut sugar, milk, flaxseed, vinegar, and vanilla until thoroughly combined, or purée in a food processor or blender.
3. In a bowl, sift together the flour, baking soda, baking powder, cinnamon, salt, and chopped walnuts.
4. Merge the dry ingredients into the wet ingredients until just combined.
5. Set about ¼ cup batter into each muffin cup and sprinkle with the topping of your choice (if using).
6. Bake for 15 to 20 minutes. The applesauce creates a very moist base, so the muffins may take longer, depending on how heavy your muffin tins are.

Nutrition:
Calories: 287 Fat: 12g Carbohydrates: 8g Fiber: 6g Proteins: 8g

236. Coconut Banana Sandwich with Raspberry Spread

Preparation time: 10 minutes **Cooking time:** 30 minutes Servings: 8

Ingredients:
French toast:

- 1 banana
- 1 cup coconut milk
- 1 teaspoon pure vanilla extract
- ¼ teaspoon ground nutmeg

Raspberry Syrup:
- 1 cup fresh or frozen raspberries
- 2 tablespoons water or pure fruit juice
- ½ teaspoon ground cinnamon
- 1½ Teaspoons arrowroot powder or flour
- Pinch sea salt
- 8 slices whole-grain bread
- 1 to 2 tablespoons maple syrup or coconut sugar (optional)

Directions:
1. Preheat the oven to 350F.
2. In a shallow bowl, purée or mash the banana well. Mix in the coconut milk, vanilla, nutmeg, cinnamon, arrowroot, and salt.
3. Dip the slices of bread in the banana mixture, and then lay them out in a 13-by-9-inch baking dish.
4. Pour any leftover banana mixture over the bread and put the dish in the oven. Bake for about 30 minutes.
5. Serve topped with raspberry syrup.
6. Heat the raspberries in a small pot with the water and the maple syrup (if using) on medium heat.
7. Leave to simmer, stirring occasionally and breaking up the berries, for 15 to 20 minutes, until the liquid has reduced.

Nutrition:
Calories: 166 Fat: 15g Carbohydrates: 7g Fiber: 4g Proteins: 5g

237. Apple Toasted Sweet Sandwich

Preparation time: 5 minutes **Cooking time:** 20 minutes Servings: 2

Ingredients:
- 1 to 2 teaspoons coconut oil
- ½ teaspoon ground cinnamon
- 1 tablespoon maple syrup or coconut sugar
- 1 apple, cored and thinly sliced
- 2 slices whole-grain bread

Directions:
1. In a large bowl, merge the coconut oil, cinnamon, and maple syrup together.
2. Add the apple slices and toss with your hands to coat them.
3. To pan fry the toast, place the apple slices in a medium skillet on medium-high and cook for about 5 minutes.
4. Cook the bread in the same skillet for 2 to 3 minutes on each side. Top the toast with the apples. Alternatively, you can bake the toast.
5. Use your hands to rub each slice of bread with some of the coconut oil mixture on both sides.
6. Lay them on a small baking sheet, top with the coated apples, and put in the oven or toaster oven at 350F (180C) for 15 to 20 minutes, or until the apples have softened.

Nutrition:
Calories: 187 Fat: 18g Carbohydrates: 7g Fiber: 4g Proteins: 4g

238. Dried Cranberry Almond Bowl

Preparation time: 10 minutes Cooking time: 0 minutes Servings: 5

Ingredients:
Muesli:
- 1 cup rolled oats
- 1 cup spelt flakes, or quinoa flakes, or more rolled oats
- 2 cups puffed cereal
- ¼ cup sunflower seeds
- ¼ cup almonds
- ¼ cup raisins
- ¼ cup dried cranberries
- ¼ cup chopped dried figs
- ¼ cup unsweetened shredded coconut
- ¼ cup non-dairy chocolate chips
- 1 to 3 Teaspoons ground cinnamon
- Bowl:

- ½ cup non-dairy milk, or unsweetened applesauce
- ¾ cup muesli
- ½ cup berries

Directions:
1. Put the muesli ingredients in a container or bag and shake.
2. Combine the muesli and bowl ingredients in a bowl or to-go container.

Nutrition:
Calories: 441 Fat: 20g Carbohydrates: 13g Fiber: 13g Proteins: 10g

239. Chocolate Banana Breakfast Bowl

Preparation time: 5 minutes **Cooking time:** 25 minutes Servings: 4

Ingredients:
- 1 cup quinoa
- 1 tsp. ground cinnamon
- 1 cup non-dairy milk
- 1 cup water
- 1 large banana
- 2 to 3 tbsp. unsweetened cocoa powder
- 1 to 2 tbsp. almond butter, or other vegan butter
- 1 tbsp. ground flaxseed, or chia or hemp seeds
- 2 tablespoons walnuts
- ¼ cup raspberries

Directions:
1. Bring the quinoa, cinnamon, milk, and water in a medium pot. Set to a boil over high heat, and then turn down low and simmer, secured, for 25 to 30 minutes.
2. Purée or press the banana in a bowl and stir in the cocoa powder, almond butter, and flaxseed.
3. To serve, set 1 cup cooked quinoa into a bowl, set with half the pudding and half the walnuts and raspberries.

Nutrition:
Calories: 392 Fat: 19g Carbohydrates: 9g Fiber: 10g Proteins: 12g

240. Fresh mint and coconut Fruit Salad

Preparation time: 5 minutes Cooking time: 5 minutes Servings: 1

Ingredients:
- 1 orange, zested and juiced
- ¼ cup whole-wheat couscous, or corn couscous
- 1 cup assorted berries (strawberries, blackberries, blueberries)
- ½ cup cubed melon (cantaloupe or honeydew)
- 1 tablespoon maple syrup or coconut sugar (optional)
- 1 tablespoon fresh mint, minced (optional)
- 1 tablespoon unsweetened coconut flakes

Directions:
1. Put the orange juice in a small pot, add half the zest, and bring to a boil.
2. Put the dry couscous in a small bowl and pour the boiling orange juice over it. If there isn't enough juice to fully submerge the couscous, add just enough boiling water to do so.
3. Cover the bowl with a plate or seal with wrap and let steep for 5 minutes.
4. In a medium bowl, set the berries and melon with the maple syrup (if using) and the rest of the zest. You can either keep the fruit cool or heat it lightly in the small pot you used for the orange juice.
5. When the couscous is soft, remove the cover and fluff it with a fork. Top with the fruit, fresh mint, and coconut.

Nutrition:
Calories: 496 Fat: 22g Carbohydrates: 7g Fiber: 14g Proteins: 11g

241. Nutty Fruity Breakfast Bowl

Preparation time: 15 minutes **Cooking time:** 30 minutes Servings: 5

Ingredients:
- 2 cups rolled oats
- ¾ cup whole-grain flour
- 1 tablespoon ground cinnamon
- 1 teaspoon ground ginger (optional)

- ½ cup sunflower seeds, or walnuts, chopped
- ½ cup almonds, chopped
- ½ cup pumpkin seeds
- ½ cup unsweetened shredded coconut
- 1¼ cups pure fruit juice (cranberry, apple, or something similar)
- ½ cup raisins, or dried cranberries
- ½ cup goji berries (optional)

Directions:
1. Preheat the oven to 350F.
2. Mix the oats, flour, cinnamon, ginger, sunflower seeds, almonds, pumpkin seeds, and coconut in a large bowl.
3. Dust the juice over the mixture and stir until it's just moistened. You might need a bit more or a bit less liquid, depending on how much your oats and flour absorb.
4. Scatter the granola on a large baking sheet (the more spread out it is the better) and put it in the oven. Use a spatula to turn the granola so that the middle gets dried out. Let the granola bake for 30 minutes.
5. Set the granola out of the oven and stir in the raisins and goji berries (if using).
6. Set leftovers in an airtight container for up to 2 weeks.

Nutrition:
Calories: 398 Fat: 25g Carbohydrates: 9g Fiber: 8g
Proteins: 10g

242. Peppery Mushroom Tomato Bowl

Preparation time: 10 minutes　　Cooking time: 15 minutes　　Servings: 1

Ingredients:
- 1 tsp. olive oil, or 1 tbsp. vegetable broth or water
- ½ cup sliced mushrooms
- Pinch sea salt
- ½ cup chopped zucchini
- ½ cup chickpeas (cooked or canned)
- 1 teaspoon smoked paprika, or regular paprika
- 1 teaspoon turmeric
- 1 tablespoon nutritional yeast (optional)
- Freshly ground black pepper
- ½ cup cherry tomatoes, chopped
- ¼ cup fresh parsley, sliced

Directions:
1. Heat a large skillet to medium-high. Once the skillet is hot, attach the olive oil and mushrooms, along with the sea salt to help them soften, and sauté, stirring occasionally, 7 to 8 minutes.
2. Attach the zucchini to the skillet.
3. If you're using canned chickpeas, wash and drain them. Press the chickpeas with a potato masher, fork, or your fingers. Add them to the skillet and cook until they are heated through.
4. Set the paprika, turmeric, and nutritional yeast over the chickpeas, and stir to combine.
5. Set in the black pepper, cherry tomatoes and fresh parsley at the end.

Nutrition:
Calories: 265 Fat: 18g Carbohydrates: 7g Fiber: 12g Proteins: 16g

243. Roasted Beets and Carrot with Avocado Dip

Preparation time: 10 minutes　　**Cooking time:** 30 minutes　　Servings: 2

Ingredients:
Avocado Dip:
- 1 avocado
- 1 tablespoon apple cider vinegar
- ¼ to ½ cup water
- 2 tablespoons nutritional yeast
- 1 tsp. dried dill, or 1 tablespoon fresh dill
- Pinch sea salt
- Roasted Veg:
- 1 small sweet potato, peeled and cubed
- 2 small beets, peeled and cubed
- 2 small carrots, peeled and cubed
- 1 teaspoon sea salt
- 1 teaspoon dried oregano
- ¼ teaspoon cayenne pepper
- Pinch freshly ground black pepper

Directions:
1. In a blender, purée the avocado with the other dip ingredients, using just enough water to get a smooth, creamy texture.
2. Alternately, you can mash the avocado thoroughly in a large bowl, then stir in the rest of the dip ingredients.
3. Preheat the oven to 350F.
4. Put the sweet potato, beets, and carrots in a large pot with a small amount of water and set to a boil. Boil for 15 minutes, until they're just barely soft, and then drain.
5. Sprinkle the salt, oregano, cayenne, and pepper over them and stir gently to combine.
6. Set the vegetables on a large baking sheet and roast them in the oven for 10 to 15 minutes, until they've browned around the edges.
7. Serve the veg with the avocado dip on the side.

Nutrition:
Calories: 335 Fat: 32g Carbohydrates: 11g Proteins: 11g Fiber: 16g

244. Raisin Oat Cookies

Preparation time: 10 minutes Cooking time: 9 minutes Servings: 2

Ingredients:
- ⅓ cup almond butter
- ½ cup maple sugar
- ¼ cup unsweetened applesauce
- 1 teaspoon vanilla extract
- ⅓ cup sorghum flour
- ⅔ cups oat flour
- ½ teaspoon baking soda
- ½ cup raisins
- 1 cup rolled oats
- ½ teaspoon ground cinnamon
- ¼ teaspoon salt (optional)

Directions:
1. Preheat the oven to 350F (180C). Line two baking sheets with parchment paper.
2. Whisk together the almond butter, maple sugar, and applesauce in a large bowl until smooth.
3. Mix in the remaining ingredients and keep whisking until a stiff dough forms.
4. Divide and roll the dough into 24 small balls, then arrange the balls in the baking sheets. Keep a little space between each two balls. Bash them with your hands to make them form like cookies.
5. Bake in the warm oven for 9 minutes or until crispy. Flip the cookies halfway through the cooking time.
6. Detach them from the oven and allow cooling for 10 minutes before serving.

Nutrition:
Calories: 140 Fat: 56.0g Carbohydrates: 224.1g Proteins: 45.5g Fiber: 30.5g

245. Oat Scones

Preparation time: 15 minutes **Cooking time:** 22 minutes Servings: 12

Ingredients:
- 1 teaspoon apple cider vinegar
- ½ cup unsweetened soy milk
- 1 teaspoon vanilla extract
- 3 cups oat flour
- 2 tablespoons baking powder
- ½ cup maple sugar
- ½ teaspoon salt (optional)
- ⅓ cup almond butter
- ½ cup unsweetened applesauce

Directions:
1. Preheat the oven to 350F (180C). Line a baking sheet with parchment paper.
2. Combine cider vinegar and soy milk in a bowl. Stir to mix well. Let stand for a few minutes to curdle, and then mix in the vanilla.
3. Merge the flour, baking powder, sugar, and salt (if desired) in a second bowl. Stir to mix well.
4. Combine the almond butter and applesauce in a third bowl. Stir to mix well.
5. Gently fold the applesauce mixture in the flour mixture, and then stir in the milk mixture.
6. Scoop the mixture on the baking sheet with an ice-cream scoop to make 12 scones. Drizzle them with a touch of water.

7. Bake in the warm oven for 22 minutes or until puffed and lightly browned. Flip the scones halfway through the cooking time.
8. Remove them from the oven and allow cooling for 10 minutes before serving.

Nutrition:
Calories: 177 Fat: 6.0g Carbohydrates: 26.6g Proteins: 5.4g Fiber: 2.5g

246. Golden Milk

Preparation time: 5 minutes Cooking time: 0 minutes Servings: 2

Ingredients:
- ½ teaspoon ground cinnamon
- ½ teaspoon ground turmeric
- ½ teaspoon grated fresh ginger
- 1 teaspoon maple syrup
- 1 cup unsweetened coconut milk
- Ground black pepper, to taste
- 2 tablespoons water

Directions:
1. Combine all the ingredients in a saucepan. Stir to mix well.
2. Heat over medium heat for 5 minutes. Keep stirring during the heating.
3. Allow to cool then pour the mixture in a blender. Pulse until creamy and smooth. Serve immediately.

Nutrition:
Calories: 577 Fat: 57.3g Carbohydrates: 19.7g Proteins: 5.7g Fiber: 6.1g

247. Mango Agua Fresca

Preparation time: 5 minutes Cooking time: 0 minutes Servings: 2

Ingredients:
- 2 fresh mangoes, diced
- 1½ cups water
- 1 teaspoon fresh lime juice
- Maple syrup, to taste
- 2 cups ice
- 2 slices fresh lime, for garnish
- 2 fresh mint sprigs, for garnish

Directions:
1. Put the mangoes, lime juice, maple syrup, and water in a blender. Process until creamy and smooth.
2. Divide the beverage into two glasses, and then garnish each glass with ice, lime slice, and mint sprig before serving.

Nutrition:
Calories: 230 Fat: 1.3g Carbohydrates: 57.7g Proteins: 2.8g Fiber: 5.4g

248. Classic Switchel

Preparation time: 5 minutes Cooking time: 0 minutes Servings: 5

Ingredients:
- 1-inch piece ginger, minced
- 2 tablespoons apple cider vinegar
- 2 tablespoons maple syrup
- 4 cups water
- ¼ teaspoon sea salt (optional)

Directions:
1. Combine all the ingredients in a glass. Stir to mix well.
2. Serve immediately.

Nutrition:
Calories: 110 Fat: 0g Carbohydrates: 28.0g Proteins: 0g Fiber: 0g

249. Easy and Fresh Mango Madness

Preparation time: 5 minutes Cooking time: 0 minutes Servings: 5

Ingredients:
- 1 cup chopped mango
- 1 cup chopped peach
- 1 banana
- 1 cup strawberries
- 1 carrot, peeled and chopped
- 1 cup water

Directions:
1. Arrange all the ingredients in a food processor, then blitz until glossy and smooth.

2. Serve immediately.

Nutrition:

Calories: 376 Fat: 22.0g Carbohydrates: 19.0g Fiber: 14.0g Proteins: 5.0g

250. Blueberry Coconut Milkshake

Preparation time: 5 minutes   Cooking time: 0 minutes   Servings: 2

Ingredients:
- 1 can coconut milk
- 1½ cups frozen blueberries
- 1 tbsp. maple syrup
- 1 tsp. vanilla extract

Directions:
1. Use a blender to mix all the ingredients until smooth. If it's too thick, add a little water. Serve immediately.

Nutrition:

Calories: 496 Fat: 22g Carbohydrates: 7g Fiber: 14g Proteins: 11g

Index

Almond Plum Oats Overnight, 7
Apple Pie Oat Bowls, 12
Apple Stew, 84
Apple Toasted Sweet Sandwich, 93
Apple-Cinnamon Breakfast Cookies, 12
Arugula Pesto Couscous, 67
Autumn Pumpkin Griddle Cakes, 21
Avocado Bagels, 14
Avocado Miso Chickpeas Toast, 8
Baba Ghanoush, 73
Baked Beans, 34
Baked Okra and Tomato, 60
Banana Cake, 83
Banana Malt Bread, 8
Banana Salad, 84
Banana Vegan Bread, 9
Barley Bake, 58
Basil Lime Green Tea, 73
Bean and Carrot Spirals, 60
Beet Balls, 68
Berries Pie, 82
Berry and Yogurt Smoothie, 73
Berry Compote Pancakes, 9
Black Bean and Mushroom Stew, 26
Black Bean Taquitos, 43
Black Beans and Rice, 58
Black Beans, Corn, and Yellow Rice, 58
Black Tea Cake, 87
Blackberry Cobbler, 87
Blueberry Coconut Milkshake, 98
Blueberry Stew, 85
Blueberry-Banana Muffins, 11
Breaded Tempeh Bites, 40
Breakfast Quinoa, 88
Broccoli Dip, 65
Buckwheat Crepes, 10
Butternut Squash, 29
Butternut Squash Chickpea Stew, 45
Butternut Squash Lasagna, 64
Cajun and Balsamic Okra, 61
Cannellini Pesto Spaghetti, 79
Cashew Zucchinis, 61
Cashew-Date Waffles, 89
Cauliflower Gnocchi, 62
Cauliflower Oatmeal, 23
Cheesy Crackers, 69
Chickpea Fajitas, 56
Chickpeas Spread Sourdough Toast, 10
Chickpeas with Harissa, 11

Chili Fennel, 61
Chinese Black Bean Chili, 34
Chocolate Almond Bars, 70
Chocolate and Nuts Goji Bars, 71
Chocolate and Walnut Steel-Cut Oats, 18
Chocolate Banana Breakfast Bowl, 94
Chocolate Chia Pudding, 19
Chocolate Protein Bites, 69
Chocolate Zucchini Bread, 24
Cilantro Coconut Pesto, 76
Cinnamon Pear Oatmeal, 16
Cinnamon Rolls, 13
Cinnamon Semolina Porridge, 21
Cinnamon-Banana French Toast, 18
Citrus-Roasted Brussels sprouts, 73
Classic Potato Comfort, 38
Classic Switchel, 97
Coconut Banana Sandwich with Raspberry
   Spread, 92
Coconut Mousse, 83
Coconut Rice, 34
Cold Cauliflower-Coconut Soup, 55
Cold Orange Soba Noodles, 79
Cooked Cauliflower Bowl, 37
Cool Mushroom Munchies, 17
Cranberry Protein Bars, 71
Creamy Brown Rice Cereal with Raisins, 89
Creamy Lentil Dip, 75
Creamy Mushroom Soup, 26
Crunchy Granola, 69
Crusty Grilled Corn, 47
Cumin Chili Chickpeas, 41
Curry Chickpea, 62
Decadent Applesauce French Toast, 21
Delightful Berry Quinoa Bowl, 17
Dried Cranberry Almond Bowl, 93
Easy and Fresh Mango Madness, 97
Easy Apple and Cinnamon Muesli, 89
Easy Collard Greens, 77
Easy Cucumber Dip, 75
Easy Italian Bowl, 37
Easy Morning Polenta, 19
English Muffins with Tofu, 16
Everyday Oats with Coconut and Strawberries, 20
Flax Crackers, 70
French Fries, 72
French Onion Soup, 25
French Potato Salad, 78
French toast, 11

Fresh mint and coconut Fruit Salad, 94
Fried Seitan Fingers, 46
Fried Zucchini, 39
Frosty Hemp and Blackberry Smoothie Bowl, 18
Fruit Infused Water, 74
Fruity Rice Pudding, 79
Garden Vegetable Stew, 32
Garlic and White Bean Soup, 57
Golden Milk, 97
Green Tea Avocado Pudding, 87
Grilled Avocado Guacamole, 47
Grilled Carrots with Chickpea Salad, 47
Grilled Margherita, 63
Hash Browns, 12
Healthy Cereal Bars, 42
Healthy Chocolate Oats Bites, 91
Hearty Pineapple Oatmeal, 17
Hemp Breakfast Cookies, 23
High Protein Toast, 7
High-Protein Salad, 52
Homemade Nutty Fruity Muffins, 91
Hot and Healthy Breakfast Bowl with Nuts, 91
Hot Wings with Ranch, 40
Hummus Carrot Sandwich, 8
Indonesia Green Noodle Salad, 79
Italian Veggie Salad, 48
Jicama and Spinach Salad Recipe, 51
Kale and Cauliflower Salad, 75
Lasagna Soup, 25
Lebanese Potato Salad, 74
Lemon Berries, 84
Lemongrass and Ginger Mackerel, 54
Lemony Quinoa, 35
Lentil Radish Salad, 51
Lentil, Lemon and Mushroom Salad, 50
Lettuce Bean Burritos, 55
Light Lemon Salad, 37
Lime Bars, 86
Lime Bean Artichoke Wraps, 64
Lime Cream, 85
Mango Agua Fresca, 97
Mango Chutney Wraps, 56
Mango Coconut Pudding, 83
Mango Mix, 85
Mango Shake, 86
Maple Sunflower Seed Granola, 90
Masala Scallops, 54
Mashed Potatoes, 54
Matzo Ball Soup, 33
Minty Apricots, 85
Mixed Berry and Almond Butter Swirl Bowl, 19
Moroccan Lentil and Raisin Salad, 22

Moroccan Vegetable Stew, 32
Multigrain Hot Cereal with Apricots, 16
Mussels in Red Wine Sauce, 52
Nutty Fruity Breakfast Bowl, 94
Nutty Morning Bread Pudding, 22
Oat Cookies, 80
Oat Crunch Apple Crisp, 68
Oat Scones, 96
Oatmeal and Raisin Balls, 67
Onion Rings, 71
PB and J Power Tarts, 13
Peach Stew, 84
Peanut Butter Muffins, 24
Pear Stew, 86
Pearl Couscous Salad, 44
Pecan Rice, 57
Peppered Pinto Beans, 60
Peppery Mushroom Tomato Bowl, 95
Pesto and White Bean Pasta, 59
Pico de Gallo, 68
Pineapple and Mango Oatmeal, 87
Pineapple and Spinach Juice, 74
Plantain Chips, 77
Potato and Kale Soup, 30
Potato Harvest Stew, 27
Pumpkin Oatmeal, 22
Quick Black Bean Chili, 27
Quinoa and Chickpeas Salad, 57
Quinoa Quiche Cups, 11
Quinoa with Vegetables, 55
Raisin Oat Cookies, 96
Ramen Soup, 30
Ranch Cauliflower Dip, 76
Raw Cashew Pesto, 76
Rhubarb and Berries Pie, 83
Roast Balsamic Vegetables, 52
Roasted Almond Protein Salad, 49
Roasted Asparagus, 72
Roasted Beets and Carrot with Avocado Dip, 95
Roasted Pepper and Tomato Dip, 80
Roasted Tamari Almonds, 66
Roasted Tomato Soup, 29
Salted Caramel Oatmeal, 89
Samosa Rolls, 14
Savory Pancakes, 15
Seasoned Tofu Potato Salad, 38
Seeds Crackers, 81
Sesame Fries, 78
Smoky Red Pepper Hummus, 66
Sour Soup, 28
Southwest Breakfast Bowl, 10
Special Cheese Board, 41

Spicy Almonds, 81
Spicy Cabbage Salad, 35
Spicy Chickpea Crunch, 36
Spicy Homemade Tortilla Chips, 42
Spicy Nut and Seed Snack Mix, 70
Spicy Peanut Ramen, 26
Spinach and Dill Pasta Salad, 48
Spinach and Mashed Tofu Salad, 49
Split Pea Soup, 28
Steak and Mushroom Noodles, 54
Sticky Rice Congee with Dates, 88
Strawberry and Chocolate Milkshake, 74
Strawberry Chia Jam, 88
Stuffed Portobello, 77
Summer Sushi, 41
Super Summer Salad, 49
Sweet and Sour Tempeh, 46
Sweet and Tangy Ketchup, 76
Sweet Potato and Black Bean Protein Salad, 50
Sweet Potato and Peanut Stew, 27
Sweet Potato Tater Tots, 80
The Best Chocolate Granola Ever, 20
Thick Sweet Potato Fries, 39
Three-Ingredient Flatbread, 42
Thyme and Lemon Couscous, 59

Tofu Nuggets with Barbecue Glaze, 60
Tofu Scramble Brunch Bowls, 13
Tofu-Spinach Scramble, 15
Tomatillo Salsa, 67
Tomato Basil Soup, 44
Traditional Indian Roti, 19
Twice-Baked Potatoes, 72
Vanilla and Apple Brownies, 82
Vanilla Flavored Whole Grain Muffins, 92
Vanilla Milk Steamer, 78
Vanilla Peach Mix, 86
Vegan Caesar Salad, 53
Vegan Curried Rice, 35
Vegan Dairy Free Breakfast Bowl, 90
Vegan Moroccan Stew, 63
Vegan Pho, 31
Vegan Tomato Soup, 44
Vegetable and Barley Stew, 31
Vegetable and Chickpea Loaf, 59
Vegetable Tacos, 43
White Bean and Broccoli Salad, 33
Wholesome Farm Salad, 36
Wonton Soup, 30
Zucchini Oatmeal, 23

Conclusion

Eating more vegan foods, by definition, will lead you to eat less saturated fat and overall calories than you would on a non-vegan diet. If you're a vegetarian or vegan or are just curious about the possibilities of plant-based nutrition, we hope that we've shown you that just because something is plant-based doesn't mean it is boring. There are so many great vegan dishes out there! Rather than being overwhelmed by everything on the market. Try to focus on the core principles of cooking with whole foods and substituting for animal products where possible. You might be amazed at how fast you gain confidence in making your recipes. Vegan food that is good for you is delicious food!

For the average adult, a diet of non-animal-based proteins and essential fats is sufficient to meet all nutritional needs.

Vegan and vegetarian diets are rich in essential fatty acids, vitamins, iron and calcium, consumed here in higher concentrations than non-vegetarian diets. Vegan foods provide all the nutrients necessary for human health. Vegan foods are entirely cholesterol-free. Vegan plant-based proteins have been shown to lower blood sugars in people with diabetes, reduce serum cholesterol levels and even alleviate arthritis symptoms.

It's radiant to get tied up in the diet trends, but if we follow the basic principles of healthy eating, we will always be on course. Consuming overflow of fruits and vegetables, whole grains, nuts, seeds and legumes, unprocessed lean protein such as beans and tofu, plenty of water and low saturated fat will be your ticket to good health. Whatever you choose to call it – vegan, vegetarian or flexitarian.

The recipes in this book are fun, delicious and inspiring! Cooking vegan food is easy. The hardest part is being consistent. You'll want to choose your ingredients wisely and be prepared to cook often. I hope that my tips encourage you to continue your plant-based journey.

Printed in Great Britain
by Amazon